Understanding Biblical Stories

COVENANT, SIN, AND REDEMPTION
IN THE OLD TESTAMENT

Ray Sutherland

Zion Press

Sutherland/Zion Press
1601 Mt Rushmore Rd. Ste 3288
Rapid City, SD 57701
www.CrossLinkPublishing.com

Ordering Information:
Quantity sales. Special discounts are available on quantity purchases by corporations, associations, and others. For details, contact the "Special Sales Department" at the address above.

Understanding Biblical Stories/Ray Sutherland. —1st ed.
ISBN 978-1-63357-353-6
Library of Congress Control Number: TBD

For Regina

Contents

Preface

"Bible stories" are sometimes wrongly thought of as peripheral to the message of the Bible. They are sometimes seen as secondary to the teachings of Jesus, the epistles, the psalms, and the better-known prophetic oracles. Because of this, the stories are often relegated to children's books and kids' Sunday school lessons. Even the label *Bible stories* brings to mind children's story time. While those uses of biblical narratives are quite legitimate and have their place, the stories themselves are much more than cute tales. Much of the Bible's most profound meaning is to be found in a proper, mature understanding of its rich and deep narratives.

Stories are theological reflections. While there is probably much historical information in them, the transmittal of those facts is not the primary purpose of the stories in the Bible. In all of the accounts, the main focus is on the works of God, and God is quite outside of the realm of historical inquiry. In other words, *Understanding Biblical Stories* only secondarily tries to undertake reconstruction of events and only if it has a bearing on the meaning of the story. The narratives are much more akin to sermons than to histories, and the examination that follows tries to showcase them in that light. *Understanding* is therefore not solely a historical study but an analysis of some of the theological meanings of the stories.

Moreover, this exegesis recognizes the useful elements of critical scholarship and incorporates them when helpful, but infrequently. While the book is not cutting-edge scholarship, it is informed by modern scholarly understandings, coupled with reverence for the Bible as God's word. The book facilitates a distinct method of approaching a text as story and uses both critical scholarship and traditional confessional understanding to illuminate the narratives chosen. The Bible's stories are powerful and meaningful. That resonance is inherent in the stories irrespective of the critical scholarly findings about them. Thus the core of this book that follows will be the thematic meaning of each account.

This study examines several of the stories from the Old Testament and interprets them in the light of some major themes: covenant, sin, and redemption. These ideas are central to the message of the Old Testament. They form the primary thrust of God's work with Israel, the chosen covenant people, and are the main interpretive tool for understanding the stories presented here. This book looks at several biblical narratives by means of these three major themes, which are intrinsic and critical to nearly the entire Old Testament.

The Old Testament contains much important theology in its own right. It is not just background to the New Testament. It is that, but it is much more. The Old Testament looks ahead to Jesus Christ, but it also points directly to God. The Old Testament makes clear that God was revealing himself to Israel and working with that nation to show much about himself in the covenant with these people.

In terms of specific books of the Old Testament, these three themes (covenant, sin, and redemption) probably first appeared as a chronological sequence in the writings of the prophet Isaiah, although the lack of structure to that book sometimes makes the sequence difficult to detect. However, it is easier to see in the Deuteronomistic history (Joshua through II Kings), which clearly makes these themes a major element in its historical theology.

In using the concepts of covenant, sin, and redemption as its main interpretive overlay, the following discussion provides a distinct lens for approaching the selected stories. This perspective is very serviceable in utilizing the stories for illustration and instruction. The audience of this book is anyone who teaches or preaches the Bible and is not intended for scholars alone. This collection of analyses will help interpreters firm up their own grasp of the texts and arrive at a better theological knowledge of the stories so as to impart it to others. A fuller understanding will assist them in unveiling additional dimensions of these specific stories and be useful as a system for navigating other narrative texts from Scripture.

Having said that, this author gives a caveat. This book proposes *some* ways of explicating the selected stories. It does not intend to establish the *one* correct meaning of any of the texts. It is important to remember that there is a nearly inexhaustible number of lessons to be learned from every Bible text, and no single reading can establish one true, definitive meaning. All biblical texts are very complex, and a myriad of messages can be unpacked from them. Therefore, to avoid premature coloring of the reader's thoughts, it is expected that one will read the selected biblical passages before delving into their specific treatment in this book. In the same vein, this study is not intended as a corrective to erroneous interpretations of the past. I have freely consulted many interpreters and have benefited from the works of others, from church fathers to contemporary theologians and philosophers. I stand on the shoulders of giants.

It is my hope and prayer that these reflections on Bible stories will be of assistance in the reading, understanding, and teaching of the eternal truths of the Bible.

Interpreting Genesis 1–3

The creation story as related in the first three chapters of Genesis has been the source of endless fascination, study, controversy, argument, speculation, and preaching; it has even been the basis for silliness and hot air at times. Some of this has been very good, some of it not so much. These three chapters are probably the most argued over part of the Bible during the past couple of centuries. The discussions regarding these chapters certainly have often generated more heat than light, and some thinkers have been more interested in attacking another position than in understanding the meaning of the text. So let's try to avoid that here and see what results from a careful reading and interpretation of the creation story.

One of the success stories of modern biblical scholarship is the detection, identification, and separation of the component sources in the Pentateuch, and the result of these efforts is the Documentary Hypothesis, which is by far the most widely held theory of Pentateuchal origins. A place at which this composite nature of the text is most clearly visible is the creation story, where there is a rather distinct shift in literary approach in chapter 2, verse 4.

The evidence for the existence in Genesis 1–3 of two distinct literary works has long been well delineated. The best known and most obvious piece of evidence is the different names of God. In Genesis 1, the Creator is called אלהים (*Elohim* or *God*), while in Genesis 2–3, the most-used name for the Creator is יהוה־אלהים (*Yahweh Elohim* or *the LORD God*). These names are quite consistent within the two narratives, with the only exception being in chapter 3 within the quotes of the conversation between the woman and the serpent, where only Elohim is used.[1]

Besides the names being different, the conceptions of God are also in contrast. In Genesis 1, God is transcendent: an unseen, intangible force who remains outside of creation and separate from it and who only has to speak to bring things into existence. The difference between creator and created is a distinction which is rigidly maintained. In 2–3, however, he enters into creation as an immanent being who forms dirt into a man, plants a garden, walks through it (prudently waiting for the cool part of the day), and is presented in generally anthropomorphic terms.

Another difference in the two distinct literary works is that Genesis 1 is tightly structured with the seven days of creation as a very clear chronological device and also has an internal structure within those seven days, which will be seen below. Genesis 2–3, on the other hand, has a feeling of timelessness, with no indications of how long a time period passes within the story, and there is no clear structure to its narrative.

In addition, the order of creation of humans is different in the two sections. In Genesis 1, humanity in general is created as the last act of creation, but in 2–3, one male is created first of all, and one female is created much later. The humans created in 1:26 seem to be a collective group all created at once while the single man created in 2:7 is a distinct individual.

Also, the chief barrier or conflicting force to creation in Genesis 1 is seen in the chaotic waters of the floods of the primordial

---

1. The actual texts are Gen. 1:1–2:4a and 2:4b–3:24. Since that is quite cumbersome, the shorthand version of *Genesis 1* and *Genesis 2–3* will be utilized.

ocean, which God must subdue and drive back. In direct contrast, aridity is the problem faced by the LORD God in Genesis 2–3, and creation cannot be effected until the LORD God brings water to the desert, which will then become the fertile earth.

Many other more subtle differences are noted in the various commentaries that scholars have presented with more or less cogency, but this basic explanation will suffice for now.

Genesis 1:1–2:4 is all but universally ascribed to the Priestly (P) source and generally thought to be the creation story by the priests of Jerusalem. Genesis 2–3 is equally widely seen as part of the Yahwistic (J) source, however, and the product of an agricultural community in the northern tribes, probably Ephraim.

Scholarship has been very successful at disassembling the creation story, along with the whole Pentateuch and a large part of the Old Testament, but the task of reassembling these pieces back into a coherent whole has only relatively recently become a priority. Scholars have done an excellent job of isolating the hypothetical J and P sections while sometimes forgetting that what we really have to work with is the completed book of Genesis in all of its combined, compiled glory. While the disentangling of parts is a very useful task, the synthesis of the components into a unified story and the understanding of the complete work are even more crucial tasks.

Disassembling a car would teach you a lot about cars, but the end result would not be a car, just a pile of parts. Only when the car is reassembled correctly do we have a whole, working automobile. However, it is true that the car is now better understood because of the dismantling. Therefore, we will make some suggestions regarding both separating the components of the creation story and then reassembling them.

The process of study which we will follow here consists of the examination of the individual strands, followed by the investigation of the meaning of the separated stories, then the reunification of them to hear the overall voice. This is the appropriate method to follow, even though much scholarship has neglected the last task. The division of the two strands is rather easily accomplished for the creation story in Genesis 1–3, and identifying verse 2:4 as the joint between the two stories is readily apparent and almost universally accepted. Each of the two stories stands alone as an independent narrative, and although we will see that together they form more than the sum of their parts, it is quite proper and necessary to look at each separately to recognize its function in the whole.

Genesis 1

We have mentioned that one of the distinctive characteristics of Genesis 1 is the close, compact seven-day structure. This design that shapes the chapter is easily seen, but verses 1–2 stand outside that structure, not referring to any particular day or time period. Literarily, verses 1–2 set the basis and framework for the story. A key to understanding these two verses is the words בראשית-ברא (*bereshiyt bara*), the translation of which is problematic. Both RSV and NRSV give a marginal alternative translation of this first verse as *When God began to create. . .* —which makes it a dependent clause appended to verse 2, in most interpretations. Choosing between the various possible translations may not be strictly necessary, but the marginal alternative highlights a factor which is important to understanding verses 1–2 as background to the seven days and as standing outside of that seven-day structure. When God began his actions to create, there was already תהו ובהו (*tohu vavohu* or *formlessness and void*) and the primordial ocean (*the deep*), which was greatly roiled by a mighty wind of God. Because there is the presence of the ocean and the wind, this interpretation has sometimes been seen as a negation of the doctrine of *creatio ex nihilo*; however, it is actually an intensification of the idea of creation from nothing, since what is being described is not something—it is not even nothing, but less than nothing. What is being described as without form and void is chaos; it is beyond nonexistence and is the opposite of existence. One of the main points of Genesis 1 is that God's intention for creation is order, but in 1:1-2, there is chaos, the opposite of order, the opposite of God's intentions.

The image of chaos portrayed through a deluge of stormy waters is a compelling one. Anyone who has ever been in a flood or in a hurricane near the coast knows the destructive force of uncontrolled water. Chaos is an accurate description of what was wrought by hurricanes Haiyan/Yolanda, Hugo, Mangkhut, Andrew, Florence, and Katrina and the 2004 tsunami and several typhoons in Bangladesh and its neighbors.

The chaos, disorder, and hostile environment of verses 1–2 are presented as the absence of God's plan and a situation which God must bring under control. It is a circumstance which must be overcome in order for creation to take place. But while the chaos of verses 1-2 is the absence of God's design, it is not the absence of God. Instead, רוח אלהים (*ruah elohim*) was over the turbulent waters. Whether רוח אלהים (ruah elohim) is translated as *spirit of God* or *wind of God*, or more loosely as *divine wind* or even *mighty wind*, it is something deriving from God and clearly reveals his presence in the chaos. God is not the cause of the chaos, nor is the chaos due to God's will, but God is there in the chaos. In the midst of the dark, watery disorder, God is present in the form of the divine wind/spirit. The tradition of interpreting this as the spirit of God is not wrong, even though a bit anachronistic. God's definite presence in the chaos is an important theological point of the combined P and J stories. The key idea is that the chaotic absence of God's *will* does not equate the absence of God himself.

Verse 3 begins the actual creation, and the first creative act on day one is the origination of light. That the making of light would be the first creative act is easily understandable to anyone who has ever been in complete darkness. The foremost desire in such situations is for light, to literally "shed some light" on the situation so that other activity can begin. Light is a prerequisite for everything else. Unrelieved darkness came with the initial chaos, but with the first day it is no longer so. Light here is a great step in creation, much more so than it seems at first. If light is a quality of existence, in contrast to the darkness of chaos, then with the creation of light, God has overcome nonexistence by creating the very reality of existence itself. There is still chaos and the watery deep, but with day one and God's creation of light, chaos and nonexistence are no longer absolute.[2]

Along with light and existence, God creates another essential aspect of the universe that same day. The onset of day and night in alternation is the beginning of time with specific periods, duration, and sequence. These had not been characteristic of the primordial chaos, and this creation of time is a major facet of God's introduction of order into his creation. Day and night are divided and arranged in a progression, and this defining and ordering forms a pattern which will be repeated throughout chapter 1. Day one is a major, dynamic step in creation and not a "slow day" as it first appears.

Darkness was a characteristic of the chaos, but it is not limited to the previous situation. Darkness is given a new place and function in creation. As a part of creation it is now under God's control and is stable, ordered. God takes an element of the chaos and makes it a useful part of things by imposing control over it and giving it divine purpose. God's transformative power takes a negative and turns it into a beautiful part of the plan ordered, stable creation-night.

Then God declares: "And it was good." This statement also is the first of what will be a pattern in chapter 1. God's imposing of existence, order, time, and light is good, and each subsequent step will be good.

---

2. John 1:1 shows this same idea when it states that *the Word* was the *light of the world*. With God's first creative word, chaos is driven back and its defeat assured. With the Word, death (chaos) is defeated by the light.

On day two, God creates the firmament, the blue dome of the sky. The firmament is envisioned here as a firm, dense, solid, waterproof dome which holds back the waters of the chaotic deep, like a bowl put into water upside down, resulting in a wet bowl, but wet only on the outside. Inside, the bowl stays dry in an air pocket where there is no water. The firmament is stable and unmoving, in contrast to the absolute instability and disorder of chaos. Once again this creative act itself is greater than the thing being physically created. God created the firmament which split the waters, and under its solidity was formed a dry space of air, a place where there is no chaos where the waters are reined in. God is again dividing and ordering, cordoning off the upper waters from the lower waters with arranged space and air in between. This space within and under the firmament is not only dry, it is a place and a situation where the waters of chaos have been driven back and defeated. In this space, within the confines of creation, God's plan, will, and design are in unchallenged control. God is victorious. There is more dividing, ordering, and creating to be done, but those acts are to be done in a systematic world, not in a formless one.

Once again, God takes an element of chaos and transforms it into a good part of his creation. This time it is the chaotic deep which is made into the ocean of creation. But the ocean stays at the bottom of the firmament and no longer is churning aimlessly. God has changed the stormy deep into the intact, cohesive, good ocean. "And it was good" comes the refrain.

During day three, God again divides and orders. This time the object being partitioned is the lower waters. Once they are restrained, dry land appears. Now there is a surface, a place for your stuff. God has again engaged in an act of creation with implications beyond the obvious. There is now a demarcation between land and sea, and it is stable, purposefully arranged, and under control, with the shore as a firm boundary between them. This sea is in contrast to the chaotic deep in that the seas of creation are under God's control. Like the darkness of chaos, God uses the waters of chaos as an element of creation by separating them, and they are afterward subject to his will in their corralled form of the earthly oceans. This makes the beach a nice place to be (except during hurricanes).

Day three also introduces another creative act which follows the literary structure of the preceding ones: "And God said, 'Let there be'. . .And there was. . .'" which appears twice here. In the second act of creation on day three, God creates plants which are living organisms and thereby crosses a major threshold. God is no longer the only living being; there is created life as well as divine, self-existent life. With this act, God establishes another pattern. Creation is given creative functions. Plants are not only alive, they are self-sustaining and propagate through seeds. Creation has been made self-perpetuating, and the these living beings are given an important role in continuing creation. God is again dividing and ordering: life from non-life. "And it was good."

On day four, God creates the heavenly bodies. At first glance, day four seems an anomaly, out of place. With the introduction of plants on day three, God had created ongoing life, and from one perspective, day four with its creation of non-living, inanimate objects in the sky seems to be an interruption of the sequence. But there are good reasons for the placement of day four and the heavenly bodies at this juncture of creation.

One reason is literary structure. The six days of creative activity have long been seen as clearly having two sections consisting of three days each. On each of the first three days, God creates an area and a situation, and on the second set of days, God fills that created area and situation with inhabitants. On day one, God created light, and on the corresponding day four the heavenly bearers and mediators of that light (stars) are created. (In the same way, days two and five, and also days three and six continue this pattern, but more on them will be discussed later.) So, we see in day four its sound purpose in the literary structure of chapter 1 in that it is the complement and completion of the work begun in day one.

Another reason for the arrangement of astronomical bodies on day four is anthropological. This part of the story is generally attributed to priests (P narrative) because those people were responsible for the precise calculation of time and the setting of religious observances according to an exact schedule based on the movements of the stars. For example, New Moon and festival days were initiated from observed astronomical events. Since the agricultural activities that the masses of common farming people in Israel would be thinking about are not timed by astronomy but by weather and other variable environmental conditions, those people were not the purveyors of the regular calculations. Accurate timekeeping was generally limited to priests (thus, we know that this section of the Bible was not written by the J narrators). All of this required careful watchfulness of the astronomical bodies for recurring patterns. Therefore, in the view of the priests, who were appointed for this astronomical awareness, monitoring, calculations, and leadership, the textual placement of the origination of the heavenly bodies is a critical element in the creation story. God's placement of the astronomical phenomena receives a day to itself because it is the first set of "inhabitants" created for that area, and therefore, like the sea and dry land, it is another base on which subsequent creation can take place. Here, God has provided the means by which humanity can maintain ritual harmony with himself and with his creation. This concept of keeping peace with creation through ritual harmony is likely a standard Semitic idea, but this particular conception of that harmony being fostered through precise calculations of time, with a divinely mandated pace and in accordance with the specific rhythms of the stars, seems to be a particularly priestly point of view and is a major support for the theory that Genesis 1 was the creation story of professional priests.

In this view, which was shared by most Semitic cultures, the priests believed that rituals were even more than keeping peace with creation—they were a monumentally necessary part of the continuation of the universe. Therefore, this is another reason that the prerequisite for proper ceremonial rites was the exact figuring of astronomical time. Indeed, the placement of the sun, moon, and stars in day four shows their important role in the maintenance of the proper working mechanism of creation. This also fits another pattern in that creatures are given a part in the sustaining of creation. Reproduction is one means by which God established this, and performance of ritual is another. In both, creatures are given a mandate to keep creation in proper balance.

Day five concerns the creation of the birds of the air and fish of the sea. They are filling the spaces that were created in day two. Again creation crosses a major threshold with the introduction of animal life, in this case non-land animals. Marine and airborne animals can act independently. They not only live but to some degree may be self-aware. In higher-order species, they may also be able to think, make decisions, and act on the basis of their decisions. Like plants, fish and birds also have a self-sustaining role in creation and propagate through eggs. This continues and extends the pattern of life seen in day three. Plants are alive; fish and birds are alive. Both sets multiply through delayed birth outside the parent's body, through seeds and eggs. Neither seeds nor eggs look anything like the parent creatures but only take on the form of the species in later development. Nevertheless, the pattern of the increasing complexity of creation has been extended with this step, up one from plants. "And it was good."

Day six contains the creation of land animals, including humans. Again we see the pattern found in the creation of life being extended to many complicated functions and advanced organisms. Land animals are not merely alive; they usually show awareness, think, and make decisions, and they propagate through a real-time birth process. Mammals especially produce live young. They do not produce something which may *eventually* become an offspring (such as seeds and eggs); they produce offspring which are *already* functioning animals and which bear an obvious resemblance to the parents. The clear classification pattern—the progression—is that each act of creating life results in life-forms which are more and more like humans, with humanity itself coming last in the structured order as the highest purpose of creation, the finishing touch.

Humanity is then the crown of creation, the goal toward which all of the preceding acts of creation were aimed. Those preliminary creative acts were preparation for the establishment of human creatures. The point of people coming last in the order of creation, in terms of theology, is twofold: first, that the fashioning of humans was the highest purpose of God's activity, and second, that God placed humanity on the earth only when it had been properly made ready for human endeavors. Following day three's enterprises, day six populates the then and there—the dry land of the moment—and also like day three, day six has two creative acts. So humans share a day with animals, highlighting the similarity between them and us and emphasizing the fact that humanity is an organic, natural part of creation. So while humans are the utmost point of creation, we are still very much an integral part of the physical dimension and not visitors or captives in a land not our own. We are not strangers in a strange land, nor outsiders who have been trapped in bodies as physical prisons. Our physical being is inherently of this natural plane and is shared with the other creatures whom God put into the world. Physically and biologically we are very similar, almost identical to the other animals, especially other mammals. Sure, we are the apex of creation, but we share a lot of fundamental characteristics with other forms of life (so don't get above yourself!).

But while humans share a day with land animals, are made of the same chemical materials, and have a markedly similar biological structure, several tremendous differences are obvious.

Humans alone are created in the image of God, and only humanity is given dominion over the earth's other inhabitants. Also, a human is the only creature who is commanded to be fruitful and multiply (although we were going to do that anyway), and only humans all certainly have free will. Each of these elements sets humanity apart within creation.

The specifics of being created in God's image are not explained, but the text clearly shows that humans are given some qualities which are derived from God and shared with him. Some of these qualities no other types of creatures possess. As much as humanity is an integral part of the created physical order, we are not totally defined or eternally bound by that order. Humanity then sits straddling the border between divinity and creature. Later Hellenistic Israelites would define this duality as humans having a soul as well as a body, which is rather true to the idea of Genesis 1, but saying that the writing of Genesis was informed by this concept would be anachronistic. Genesis 1 does not attempt to delineate this notion of spiritual versus animal traits further and leaves it enigmatic. But while we are left uncertain as to exactly *which* qualities we have that come from God's essence, it is clear at this point in the text that we at least possess some.

The idea of humans having dominion over the earth is probably related to the concept of being created in God's image, although the only direct textual connection between the two is sequential. Humans are given power, but it is delegated power. In a happy coincidence, the traditional translation of the Hebrew root רדה (*radah*) has been the English word *dominion*, which has less of the idea of ruling and dominating than does רדה (radah). The English concept of dominion probably comes closer to the idea being propounded in Genesis. The feudal concept of dominion was a two-way concept, with the person having dominion possessing authority over the domain but remaining responsible to a higher lord for the way in which that authority was exercised. In other words, feudal dominion was not absolute authority but authority from the higher lord, whose own authority and policies had to be respected and carried out as a part of exercising dominion. Humans are given that sort of dominion, not absolute authority. We have control over the earth, but final say rests with God, and we are responsible to him for our exercise of the dominion we are given.

The belief in humans having this dominion handed down by God, with whom we share control of the created world, was a distinct departure from the early Semitic standard theology of humanity. This standard is probably best represented by the Babylonian *Enuma Elis* in which humanity is created as an afterthought and exists primarily in order to feed and care for the gods as they deserve.

Humanity having dominion over the earth's inhabitants, being made in the image of God, and multiplying fruitfully as male and female and filling the earth made creation complete. The finished creation was more than the sum of its good parts; the totality of creation was no longer simply good. "It was *very* good."

And on the seventh day God rested. So say the traditional translations. This is quite an accurate and acceptable translation and quite in accord with standard usage. But like many translations, it is incomplete. The Hebrew word translated as *rest* is שבת (*shabbat*), from which we get the loan-word *sabbath*. Since the word has come into English, we may be able to better understand the verse by simply leaving the word in Hebrew and reading it as "In the seventh day God *sabbathed* with the work which he had done."[3] Sabbath is indeed a day of rest, but it is also a day of worship with people joining in spiritual communion with God.

---

3. This requires an explanation of some creative use of prepositions. The preposition מן (*min*) which is used in 2:2 is usually translated as *from*, which fits better with *resting from*. But translating prepositions is inexact at best, and the discrepancy can easily be seen as one of the visible joints between the two stories. The overall impact of the seventh day is quite compatible with the interpretation offered here, even if some technicalities differ.

In this translation, we are less likely to see a tired God who needs a day off and more likely to see the seventh day as Genesis 1 intended: a Sabbath day of communion among God, humanity, and all creation. Day seven is a Sabbath of respite, but it is also a Sabbath of perfection and the recognition of that perfection. It is God, humans, and the physical word in perfect harmony, perfect peace, perfect equilibrium. God and his works were in interlocking psychic relationship. "God's in his heaven, all's right with the world" was reality and not a pipe dream. While humans were the final creative act and acme of creation, the Sabbath day is in another sense the final purpose of God's creation. Not just existence and being, but existence with total completeness and harmony within each part and among all of the parts as interdependent with God.

Day seven as the Sabbath of perfection and communion is fitting in two ways. It is the climax of the progression of creation throughout the chapter. To summarize, the trajectory begins with the negative existence of chaos. Then on the first day, existence, light, and time are created. Next, the firmament drives back the watery deep, removing chaos, followed by dry land being covered by plants on day three. Heavenly bodies for keeping track of days and seasons are created on day four, and day five populates the sea and sky with fish and birds, respectively. Land animals followed by people appear on day six, and with humanity creation reaches its height. The Sabbath, day seven, is the resulting wonderful situation in which all is right: every piece of God's work is in its proper place, fulfilling its correct function in perfect working order, and the whole of creation is in complete harmony with itself and with God. The progression has reached its logical and ultimate end. Completion, perfection, communion. Sabbath.

The other way in which the Sabbath is a fitting conclusion is in terms of literary structure. As already said, days one through three each see the creation of a place or a situation, and days four through six each see that situation or place populated and filled. It seems that only day seven has no corresponding day. But day seven has its counterpart in the chaos of verses 1–2. Yes, the correspondence between these two is quite different in type from the correspondence between the two sets of days and can be diagrammed as the following:

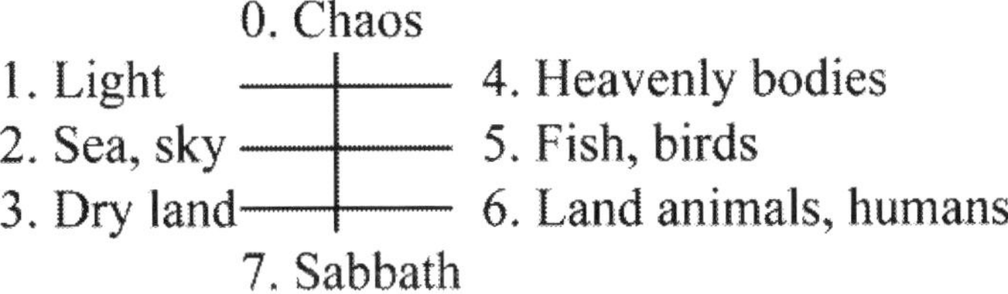

The correspondence between chaos and Sabbath is perpendicular to the horizontally correspondent days, but both sets of correspondence reflect the increasing complexity, roundedness, and goodness of the creation. The correspondences between the first three days and the second set show completion and fulfillment with each day being the other's complement in the pair. Chaos and Sabbath are not complementary but diametrically opposed, and this shows the contrast between the lack of God's will and the full attainment of that will.

Another aspect of Genesis 1 often noted is the abstract concept of God in the chapter. Although God is the major character, he only speaks things into being, never appearing in any visible form building his creations. In fact, he remains entirely offstage as an intangible and supernatural presence only. Although he is not aloof to his people and ends his work week by engaging in Sabbath, God in this section of the creation story is transcendent, outside of creation in the sense that he is not in any way defined by creation and derives none of his being from it. He truly is wholly other. This portrayal is frequently thought to be the priestly view of God, the result of long hours of intellectual reflection by an ancient priestly class with theological training and leisure to ponder it, and so furnishes additional proof that this chapter is part of the P, not J, narrative.

Genesis 2–3

The second section of the Genesis creation story, the J narrative, also begins with a problem to be solved but puts into play a literary approach and plot resolution quite different from what we've seen. As was said already, in Genesis 1, the problem was water and chaos in the form of the deep, chaotic, unordered flood. In Genesis 2, the problem is exactly opposite—aridity; there is no water to make things grow. Here in Genesis 2, the LORD God causes an אד (*ed*) of water or water vapor to go up from the land so that growth can take place.[4] This event takes place outside a chronological framework since the story refrains from mentioning a specific time; all of it takes place in a timeless setting but with a definite element of internal time, duration, and sequence involved.

Next the LORD God formed a man from the "dust of the ground" and made the man live. The story aspect of this creative act seems very different from the majestic abstraction of Genesis 1 where God simply speaks humanity into being and in his own image. In the corresponding view of Genesis 2, we humans are just dirt—dirt that breathes. But there is much more to the theology of the story, of course. We are dirt, but dirt that was formed by God's own hands; the LORD God actively shapes the dust that becomes the man. God takes direct action and is very personally involved. The idea of יצר (yetzer or formed) is that God constructed the man himself, using his own hands like a potter. The creation of the man occupies the LORD God's full engagement and attention. God is willing to get directly involved

---

4. The exact meaning of אד (ed) is unknown, but it refers to some form of water. Whatever the precise meaning, the land is now well watered, and additional creation can be carried out.

and literally get his hands dirty to form the man correctly and lovingly. It is literally a hands-on project. Obviously, God in Genesis 2–3 is a God who really gets into his work! The man is formed from dust, from earthly material. Just like the representation in the P manuscript, the idea is that we are from inception a deliberate part of creation, and we belong here by God's design. But humans are not limited by their physical being. We are made of dust and dirt that breathes, but oh, what wonderful breath we have! The breath in the man was not just air. It is God's own being within us, and a major part of our life stems from God himself. This is much closer theologically to the idea of humans being created in God's image even though the literary presentation is radically different. Genesis 1 makes the point as an abstract theological category while Genesis 2 makes the point much more subtly—as a part of a plot element. However, in both, humanity is given qualities which derive from God, and so we share with him some of his identity, even while we are also organically a part of physical creation. This is an important clue to seeing how the two stories work together even though they evince very different literary devices.[5]

That we are a fiber of the structure of creation shows us that this earthly physical life is important. Life here, in the representation set forth in Genesis, is not just preparation for the next world (although it doesn't preclude that life here is that, too), nor a burden to be borne, nor a soiled garment to be discarded, much less is earthly life merely "flesh" which must be "mortified." Our earthly, corporeal life is a gift from God and very good in its own right.

Although normal anthropology is unable to find a Greek-style reference to soul in the Hebrew Scriptures, Genesis 1–3 as a unit fits the idea of spirit quite well. The concepts of רוח אלהים (ruah elohim) which is literally translated "wind of God" which

---

5. Ps. 33:6 ties both concepts together: "By the word of the Lord the heavens were made, and all their host by the breath of his mouth."

moved over the face of the waters in chapter 1 and God having "breathed into his nostrils the breath of life" do not refer to spirit or soul in any technical sense but show a very clear and definite difference between divine and physical substance, with contact between the two being limited but clear and with humanity being the focal point of that contact.

The LORD God also gets very intimately involved in making a particular home for the man when God plants a garden. Here the LORD God makes provision for humanity by planting trees, and we see God the farmer. Interestingly, the story makes a point that the trees not only produce edible material but also fruit that is pleasant to eat, and the trees themselves are aesthetically pleasing as well. God builds beauty into creation as well as utility; we see God the aesthete. Creation is not only functional but enjoyable and attractive as well. Again we see that physical life is good and important in its own right, by God's original design.

Note the sequence of events in Genesis 2. God first created a human and then creates what the human needs. Creation is tailored to the perceived needs of the man who already is on the scene. While the narrative action is different from that of Genesis 1, there is again a great similarity in theology. In both, humanity is the central aim of creation, and God effects creation to meet the requirements of humanity. But the plots diverge from one another: Genesis 1 has humans appear only when the world has been properly prepared; in the reverse order, Genesis 2 has the human brought forth first so that his needs can be assessed and then met accurately and efficiently.

Verse 15 makes clear that the LORD God gives the man a task in the garden, and while the garden is intended to provide food for the man, he is given the work of tilling and keeping it. The man was not intended for a life of idleness, and work was a part of the LORD God's intention for humanity from the beginning. Labor did not come about because of the fall and the curse but was a natural outcome of the goodness of the garden surroundings and of the blessing of life in God's presence. The blessing included not just work but *hard* work, as any orchard owner or peach picker will quickly attest. Admittedly, the fall and curse perverted the work of humanity and made it drudgery and rendered work less productive, but work itself, and especially working at a set of tasks ordained by the LORD God, was initially an integral part of the bliss of creation in its perfect state in the garden.

The garden also contains the seeds of tragedy: the tree of life and the tree of the knowledge of good and evil, which are in the midst of the garden. These trees are the subject of a command to obey God and not eat of the fruit from certain places. The imperative is a boundary for the man. To be human is to be limited by physical boundaries and by behavioral restrictions. Some things are not possible, and some things are not permitted. The underlying concept is quite similar to an element of Genesis 1 which is the proper dividing, ordering, and structuring of creation with everything in its proper place fulfilling its appropriate function. Human freedom must be set aside from the prohibited actions. God is the creator, and humanity is the created who must live within the divinely ordained decree. The results of disorder are clearly stated by God, and the result is death. Life is possible only within God's standards, and life experienced within that order and those boundaries is very good. But the story of Genesis 2–3 makes clear that disobedience is possible. Humans are independent moral agents, and decisions can and indeed must be made freely by humans.

We can also note the implicit presence in both stories of a major theme of the Bible: covenant. *Covenant* is the standard translation of the Hebrew word ברית (*beriyt*), which could with equal accuracy be translated as *treaty, contract, bargain,* or *deal.* But since covenant sounds more religious and high class, it is the most often-used translation. One of the key elements of the Old Testament is God's covenant with Israel. "I will be your God and you shall be my people" is the most succinct version of the covenant with the full version being the whole Torah. Here it is a specific contract with humanity—God will provide for them, and they will obey God. In Genesis 2 we see a covenant clearly in the statement in verses 16–17, where the man is allowed to eat all he wants from the garden, but he is not to eat from the tree of the knowledge of good and evil.

God saw that it was not good for the man to be alone and knew that humans are social beings, who need to be a part of a community in order to engage in interpersonal interaction. In first response to this need, the LORD God created animals. He formed them out of the ground, and therefore the animals, like humans, are integrally part of creation, but he does not impart his breath into animals, so the man alone is invested with that characteristic. The man has God's breath in him; the animals do not. This results in the animals being brought to the man who then names them. This is a theological concept which is closely parallel to the dominion given to humanity in Genesis 1. In Israelite thought, the authority to confer names constituted power over the named. Parents name children, and in II Kings 23:34, when Pharaoh Neco places Eliakim on the throne of Jerusalem, he changes Eliakim's name to Jehoiakim, an insignificant linguistic difference but a significant imposition designed to manifest Pharaoh's authority over the new king. The man's naming of the animals is delegated to him by the LORD God and shows that the animals are a subset of his domain. This again is similar theologically to Genesis 1 but very different in terms of plot and literary presentation.

But none of the animals provide the full degree of companionship which would complete the man. All were good; some were useful; dogs are good companions but short on conversation; some were puzzling (giraffes prove that God has a sense of humor). None was the helpmate which the man needed.

So the LORD God created a woman who was precisely what would be the perfect complement to the man. They were socially and psychologically compatible, being of one flesh, and were in sum a perfect match. God gave them to each other; they desired one another, and their nakedness was not a source of shame. The two humans lived in a state of perfect concord and communion between themselves, between themselves and God, and between themselves and creation. Eden is therefore a state of idyllic, comprehensive harmony very comparable to the Sabbath idea of Genesis 1. This similarity is a major connection between the two narrative threads and serves as a literary means of joining the two sections of the creation story. "And it too was very good. . ."

For a while. The commandment not to eat of the tree of the knowledge of good and evil contains within it the innate possibility of disobedience or at least the temptation to do so. The snake in the story is a personification of that temptation. One of the keys to understanding the snake in these terms is in two parts. First, the snake makes no statements which are factually untrue. He beguiles, but he does not lie. The snake does not even overtly persuade; he only points out possibilities. Second, this telling of misleading truth applies to his incomplete statement of the consequences, which, while generally deceptive, is technically true and contains a key theological idea of the text: sin is the sure result of humans trying to take the place of God.[6] "You will be like God [or gods] (אלהים or elohim), knowing good and evil," was the serpent's bona fide statement but incomplete because it ignores the deadly repercussions of that knowledge. The snake's statement "Ye shall not surely die" (Genesis 3:4 KJV) is also not technically untrue since it could well be translated as *you will not immediately die*, or *you will not completely die* (infinitive +

---

6. This is more fully treated in Ronald A. Veenker, "Do Deities Deceive?" in Bill T. Arnold, Nancy L. Erickson, and John H. Walton (ed.), *Windows to the Ancient World of the Hebrew Bible: Essays in Honor of Samuel Greengus* (Winona Lake, IN: Eisenbrauns, 2014), 208-211.

imperfect = intensifier).[7] The serpent's implication is that God is deliberately and unnecessarily keeping the pair in a state of ignorance and withholding knowledge which is rightly theirs.[8] The serpent's words have the effect of lessening their faith in God's ultimate goodness and his authority.[9] The man and woman are then faced with a decision whether to continue to rely on God and his instructions or to initiate their own efforts outside of God's plan—in effect to become their own gods.

The sin that followed was a conscious act by the humans and a decision in which they had ample time to consider beforehand. The snake did not make them do it. It may have manipulated them indirectly, but he neither coerced them nor overtly duped them with falsehoods. The decision to disobey was theirs alone and was a willful, premeditated one. They intentionally and quite knowingly grasped what was forbidden, crossed a prohibited boundary, and attempted to usurp God's place, disastrously.

The immediate effect was their awareness of their nakedness, which serves in the story as a symbol for the consequences of sin. The couple suddenly wanted to hide their different bodies from each other. This shows that one of the upshots of their sin was a broken relationship between them as man and woman. Now their nakedness is a source of embarrassment, and they feel

---

7. R. J. Williams, *Hebrew Syntax: An Outline* (Toronto: University of Toronto Press, 1976), 37–38.

8. The existence of the chaotic deep and the snake's attitude lead to the puzzling idea that there is some force separate from and external to God that is hostile to God and his will. This is not addressed in the text, but the conclusion is nearly inescapable. In a similar vein the trees in the midst of the garden also seem to possess a power independent of God. While in historical-critical terms, these may be simply explained as remnants of an earlier, more mythic version of the stories, such speculation fails to address the meaning in the present text of these ideas which seem to be mystifying anomalies. Rev. 21:1 seems to share this idea of the deep as a hostile power ("no more sea"), and extends it symbolically to the earthly oceans.

9. Nowhere in Gen. 3 is the snake presented as anything but a snake. The later identification of it as Satan is without textual warrant in Genesis.

the need to partially avoid one another. The man's great joy and exuberance at meeting the woman turn to evasiveness and blaming. The "flesh of my flesh" has become the "woman [who] gave to me of the tree" and resultant sin. They have lost their trust in one another, and guilt and shame have replaced the closeness, desire, and joy of their lives. Instead of naked and unashamed, they now try to cower behind leaves.

Because of the broken relationship, they hide not only from each other but from God, too. When they hear God's voice in the garden, they try to elude him, but they learn the biblical principle that God always wins at hide and seek. God's subsequent meeting with them reveals the tragedy and the finality of the sin.[10] They have transgressed the boundaries between themselves and God and can therefore no longer abide in God's direct presence. The relationship with God is broken by their sin. Because of their disobedience they are banished and must end their close association with God, leaving the garden where they had walked and talked with him previously. The closeness of the man's relationships has soured into nastily blaming both the woman and God; the man's expression "the woman which you gave me" is his attempt to blame the woman and God. Servitude, dejection, guilt, and anxiety now replace the peace, freedom, and innocence of life in the garden. Fragmentation, hurting, are now the hallmarks of life instead of the harmony, communion, and goodness intended by God.

God then pronounces the punishments for the transgression. Agriculture changes from pleasant tilling and keeping to pulling weeds, thorns, brutally hard work, and failed crops. Childbirth

______

10. The writer uses an excellent plot device here. The questioning and inposition of punishment highten the tension from the question of whether the humans will die immediately or not. This is also more fully treated in Ronald A. Veenker, "Do Deities Deceive?" in Bill T. Arnold, Nancy L. Erickson, and John H. Walton (ed.), Windows to the Ancient World of the Hebrew Bible:Essays in Honor of Samuel Greengus (Winona Lake, IN: Eisenbrauns, 2014), 212-213.

ceases to be a blessing as in 1:28 and is now a curse of excruciating labor. The snake loses its legs, has to eat dirt, and humans will fear, hate, and kill them ever afterward.

But the worst result is not any of these punishments imposed by by God. By far the worst effect of the fall is the natural consequence of disobedience which is the loss of the close relationsip which had existed between the man, the woman, and God. God had been directly visible to them in the garden while they had been sinless but now the fallen humans wished to evade God, rejecting him. This loss is clearly seen in their having to leave the garden. God does not impose this penalty on them as a harsh punishment, nor does he, in a rage, drive them out of his sight. God's eviction of them from the garden was not vengeance but mercy. Once they have become sinful, the humans coming into God's presence would have resulted in their complete destruction.[11] The cherubs which God placed at the garden were not just to protect the garden but to protect the humans from entering and being annihilated.

All of the pain is not on the part of the man and the woman. In the garden, God calls out "Where are you?" in 3:9 when the man and the woman are hiding from him, and this can be read as a plaintive cry of desolation due to the absence of the man and woman. It can be equated to the feeling of a parent frantically searching for a lost child. There are similar statements elsewhere in the Bible of God's sadness at being abandoned by his people. The first is found in Jeremiah 14:17–18:

> You shall say to them this word: Let my eyes run down with tears night and day, and let them not cease, for the virgin daughter—my people—is struck down with a crushing blow, with a very grievous wound. If I go out into the field, look— those killed by the sword! And if I enter the

---

11. Ex. 33:18–23: I Kings 8:10–11 also contain this premise.

city, look—those sick with famine! For both prophet and priest ply their trade throughout the land, and have no knowledge.

The second is found in Hosea 11:8-9:

How can I give you up, O Ephraim? How can I hand you over, O Israel? How can I make you like Admah? How can I treat you like Zeboiim? My heart recoils within me; my compassion grows warm and tender. I will not execute my fierce anger; I will not again destroy Ephraim; for I am God and no mortal, the Holy One in your midst, and I will not come in wrath.

In these texts God is clearly in emotional distress because of Israel's sin and disloyalty and the subsequent rupture of the covenant. God's manifestations and his perfect relationship with them, the tranquil harmony of all of creation in communion with God, the Sabbath which he had enjoyed in relaxed fellowship with his children—all were ruined in a matter of moments by human sin. This could possibly be read as implying that the humans' sin caused God greater pain than it caused them.

A major consequence of the sin and the most obvious one is the initiation of death, as stated by God in chapter 2:17 when he prohibits the eating of the fruit: "In the day that you eat of it you shall die." Yet, as the serpent predicted, their lives did not end on the day they made the terrible mistake to eat it. Genesis 5 tells us that Adam lived for 930 years, and Eve lived to have at least three sons. Either God got it wrong, or the death he warned them about was not simply the cessation of life. Like everything else in this seemingly simple story, it is much more complicated and subtle than it seems on the surface. The man and the woman did not die on the day they ate the forbidden fruit (although eventually they did die). Instead, their lives outside the garden were much reduced—sorrowful, pale shadows of the wonderful lives they had had in the garden. The death that God had warned them about was not just the termination of life but the tremendous lessening of life. The death resulting from sin included the terms of the curse pronounced by God. Because of their sin, their life became back-breaking work, briars, agonizing birth, the murder of a son, and life generally and badly out of balance and messy. In other words, the death which their sin caused was the reintroduction of chaos into creation, a regression. The work of God in chapter 1 in defeating and driving out chaos was partially undone by the humans in chapter 3 by their sin. The words of God that death would come on that fateful day were correct, and their lives became the living death outside of God's direct presence and will. The words of the snake are then revealed as a cruel lie, even though factual; their lives did not end in an ultimate sense, but the goodness and richness of their days entwined with God withered in slow decay, the disintegration of sin. They had become like God in knowing good and evil, but their knowledge came by tasting evil of their own making.

The immediate effect of sin was the humans becoming aware of their nakedness which, in literary terms, is emblematic of their sinful state. Their natural impulse to clothe themselves shows their awareness of their sin and the need to eliminate the results of the disobedience. Their attempt to make aprons of fig leaves was completely inadequate. That their impulse to cover themselves, seeking atonement, was correct is confirmed when God provided garments of skin which adequately clothed them. [12] This reveals the important theological principle that sinful humans cannot effect atonement for themselves, it takes God's actions to accomplish that.

---

12. The Hebrew word for *to cover* (כפר or *kafar*) is the word also used for *to atone*. Their attempts to cover their sin are seen in the story as a move to make up for it. This word does not appear in Gen. 3, but the concept does.

One of the main differences between the failed human attempt to effect atonement and God's successful one is that the tree providing the leaves was not killed while the animal providing the skin died. God had told the man regarding the forbidden tree "in the day that you eat of it you shall die." Therefore, God's statement that death (in the form of the ending of life) would occur on the day they ate from the tree is proven to be true. But the man and the woman who sinned were not who the ones who physically died. The death happened to an animal instead. The animal was a totally blameless casualty who died for the humans' sins. God's love for the man and the woman was such that the death they had earned, deserved, and brought on themselves was diverted onto an innocent victim who suffered the death which the humans' deserved. The death caused by sin could not be averted, but it could be deflected through God's love, grace, and provision of the substitutionary victim for atonement.[13]

Here we see a clear depiction of the Israelite theology of sacrifice. God's killing of the animal for its skin is the first sacrifice, but the animal did not die for God's direct benefit, nor was it given to God. The animal died because the man and woman had sinned and needed redemption. God bought their atonement at the cost of a blameless creature's life. In the same way, Israelite sacrifice involved the death of an innocent animal whose death secured the atonement and redemption of the worshiper. The sacrifice was not a gift to God (who didn't need a dead sheep, anyway) but was the death necessitated by the worshiper's sin—which broke their relationship with God and which only a death could restore.

Redemption was achieved, but there was a cost, which was borne by God who lost one of his animals, and by the animal who died.

---

13. Paul was being Israelite and not specifically a Christian when he said "The wages of sin is death" (Rom. 3:23).

Adam and Eve could no longer walk and talk with God as they had in the garden. Now their sin had shattered that harmony. But due to God's grace and mercy, their lives did not simply end. Life continued—lesser life, but life. God was no longer directly present with them, but neither was he wholly absent. They no longer had the close friendship of the garden, but there was still a weaker connection. Now their relationship was a more distant one, based on worship from afar and sacrificial death. Nonetheless, God was still a presence in their lives, and even fallen life could contain some blessings as well as curses.

We also see another, possibly the greatest, example of God converting an element of chaos into part of his will. Death is the terrible, awful result of sin and is also inescapable. But God miraculously turns the death into redemption. "The wages of sin is death" is true, but the gift of God is that the death of the innocent sacrificial victim becomes the instrument of redemption. The death of a stand-in becomes the centerpiece of Israelite worship and the primary mediator of God's presence; because of the transforming act of God, death is changed from the ultimate loss of his presence to the means of reentering it.

Reassembly

While the differences between the two literary components of Genesis 1–3 are clear, we have also seen some important similarities in theological concepts. *Created in God's image* from the first narrative matches *God-breathed life* from the second. *Dominion over creation* matches *naming of the animals*. Humanity is the highest purpose of creation in both. In addition to these matching details, we can also see an even more important theological connection when we examine the stories as a unit. Specifically, the two stories work together very well in presenting an integrated theology of creation, humanity, covenant, sin, and redemption.

The plot structure of the combined stories shows a strong, close correspondence to the standard structure of classical drama. In particular, it is the same as the conventional five-act structure of the plays of Terence and Shakespeare (among other authors). One system of labeling these five acts, which is still widely used and recognized today, names each act in order as: setting, rising action, climax, falling action, resolution. We can see this same structure and pattern in the two interwoven stories of Genesis 1–3.

The setting, which provides a perspective from which to see and understand the subsequent actions, is contained in 1:1–2. This passage sets the scene by showing what the absence of God's order, the absence of God's will, entails: chaos, destruction, and darkness. Next, the rising action is contained in the six days of creation, in which God brings existence and order resulting in a world that is orderly, harmonious, and good. The action rises in that each act of creation brings the world closer to finished creation. The climax is found in day seven and the perfection of Eden. The Sabbath/Eden perfection is also the joint or seam which holds the two sections of the story together: Sabbath and Eden, where life and existence are orderly, right, and harmonious. God sabbaths with humanity and creation, and it is very good. This situation is also an accurate description of life in the garden for the man and the woman. They are naked and unashamed and walk and talk in the garden—with each other and with God—and all creation is a harmonious whole. But the origins of tragedy is present in the form of the tree of the knowledge of good and evil. The perfection of Sabbath in Eden has the tree in its midst.

The falling action is the temptation, the sin, the hiding, the sewing of fig leaves, and the confrontation with a now remote God. The man and the woman, like the action, have *fallen* from what was perfect now to chaos and death. The resolution (or *catastrophe* in tragedies, and this certainly is one) is the discovery by God, the imposition of punishment, and the departure from the garden for the mess and confusion of the fallen world.

The combined stories present a much more complete theology of creation than either of them does alone. The two stories' dramatic structure, similar to the archetypal five-act play, may be diagrammed as follows:

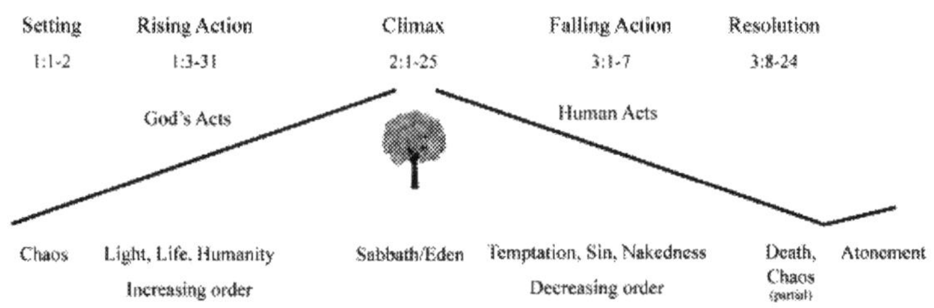

In this combined view, Genesis 1 shows God transforming chaos into Sabbath perfection by dividing and ordering. Genesis 2 presents that creation in its perfect harmony as God intended. Genesis 3 shows human sin, causing God's perfect creation to fall back into (partial) chaos. But that reemerging chaos again gives way to God's control because of God's provision of grace and forgiveness. The narrative line of rising and falling action with resultant denouement provides a logical shape for the themes of covenant, sin, and redemption. This section of the Bible, the creation account, will be important in understanding many of the stories in the Old Testament with the same theological structure.

To summarize the thematic threads, God established a *covenant* with the man and the woman by providing them with initial life and then the garden, which contained the necessities for continued life. In return they were to obey God and refrain from eating from the tree of the knowledge of good and evil. Yet *sin* entered the world when the man and the woman made the decision to eat from the forbidden fruit and broke the covenant, thereby earning death. *Redemption* was the unearned gift of God to the humans, enabling them to continue to live, even though in a reduced state. But there was a cost to forgiveness in that the animal had to die. The death earned by the humans was diverted onto the innocent victim.

The two stories sewn up together are a *gestalt* and together constitute much more than the sum of the parts. A concept of God much greater than found in either story alone is presented. The transcendent God who speaks the world into being in 1 and the immanent LORD God of 2-3 who forms man with his own hands, breathes life into him, and walks with him in the garden are both characteristics and aspects of the same God. Creation as a process is good, and finished creation is *very* good. Human enjoyment of the physical reality and variety of creation is also good; however, sin has perverted the design, and this alludes to the idea that much that is good can become evil when misused.

A particular point which requires the stories to function as a combined unit in order to be understood concerns the chaos of the setting in 1:1–2 and the chaos of fallen human life outside the garden in a later verse. Genesis 1:2 makes a special point that in the תהו ובהו (tohu vavohu or formless and void) chaos, something of God was, however, undeniably there. Whether we translate רוח אלהים (ruah elohim) as spirit of God or wind of God or even as divine wind, the clear point is that God himself was present in that chaos. Chaos is the absence of God's will; it is not the absence of God. When the humans entered the fallen world outside of the garden, they were not entering a chaos bereft of God's presence. God is there in chaos as well as in Sabbath and Eden.

We see that the combined story ends on three hopeful notes which are closely related. The first one is the institution of sacrifice and God's loving and gracious provision for atonement and the continuing of a partial relationship with humanity through worship. The man and the woman did not die the day they ate of the forbidden fruit because God made room for their restoration (even if not to the previous state of things). God's allocation for and flexibility with his sinful humans are critical elements of a series of connected themes (covenant, sin, and redemption) which form a message paramount in the entire Bible. Even stories which do not specifically present this pattern are integral parts of a larger complex which does.[14]

The second hopeful point is that even in the cataclysm of fallen existence, God was still there, and *fallen* life as *fallen* people outside the garden in the *fallen* world was still a life in which the blessings of God's presence and of relating in some way with him were still possible. God is around in a lesser, indirect way, but he remains caring and involved. The absence of God's original plan is not the absence of God.

Another positive facet of the combined stories is that the fall, sin, and reintroduced version of chaos are not said to revoke God's judgment that his creation is very good. However compromised, reduced, and scarred it may be, creation is still God's work, still very good, and still able to bear good things and possibilities. Within the chronological and developmental progression through chaos, Sabbath, Eden, fall, reintroduced chaos, and beyond, God is attending in all his power and love. In the dual story of Genesis 1–3 we see the confirmation of the famous words of an unknown but great theologian: "God is great; God is good. . ."

---

14. Some of the stories of David before he became king do not readily lend themselves to this interpretation, but they form an important part of his life as a whole which certainly fits the overarching pattern very well.

Cain and Abel

After the fall. . .Life in a fallen world: pain, suffering, and sickness. Failed crops and failed dreams. Gloominess, drudgery, hunger, weariness, and despair. Life in the living death of chaos. But still, it was life. Adam and Eve's sin had taken away God's nearness and much more from them, but it hadn't taken away his parental love for them, nor did it remove his grace. His beneficence left them with their physical life and his indirect presence. And they still had the determination to survive and make the best of it. They still had God's gifts of love for each other and hope. Their love and hope combined had the same result for them that it has had for so many of God's people—a baby.

The arrival of the babies and their continued life showed that while the first humans were no longer in God's direct presence, God was not absent. As God had been present in the primordial chaos of Genesis 1:1–2, he was likewise in the swirling chaos of their life in a fallen world. Life outside of God's plan isn't life outside of God's care. He was yet very much at work in their world and in their lives. God was with them in a diminished way, but he was still there, still loving them, still guiding them, and still blessing them. The first babies were clearly a sign of that. The arrival of a healthy baby is always an occasion for joy, and those of the world's original infants certainly were such joyous occasions. Eve recognized the hopeful nature of the baby's coming. Her statement that with the LORD's help she had gotten a baby shows us that she clearly saw the nature of God's love in this event. Just as that tiny individual child was a reassuring indication for Eve that her life would go on, the general patterns of life, procreation, and birth are all unambiguous signs of God's proximity, affection, and involvement. Yes, that intervention is more felt through faith than seen and perceived by direct knowledge, but Adam and Eve knew that the births of Cain and Abel were evidence of God still at work in their lives, proof that they were not alone and forsaken. Eve's statement is acknowledging that life goes on through means of natural processes but that God is the empowering force behind those processes. The first couple had their part to play in the conception and birth, but their role was effective only through God having a hand in it.

The couple's expulsion led to the loss of God's being visible to them, but it did not cause God to abandon his people. God remains heavily involved in people's lives, and because of God's presence, creation still functions largely as it was intended and designed to operate. As in Eden, God was in a covenant relationship with humans in which he provided the requisite materials and methods by which the humans could secure the necessities of life. Because of this, Cain and Abel were able to herd and to farm, and, through God's created natural processes and his continued approval, their efforts yielded results. The two brothers were able to survive through their work, involving the nurturing of God's creatures. In the spring, Cain's seeds sprouted, and Abel's ewes brought forth lambs. Those types of things had happened before the fall and continued afterward. God's goodness, as reflected in the virtue of the natural processes of creation, was still at work, and, even though adulterated, humanity could still know God's providence through the growth and increase of his creatures—from which humans reaped the benefit.

The provision God made in Eden for the forgiveness of sin through sacrifice remained in place and humanity was still able to approach God through the institution of worship and the offering of sacrifice. Cain's produce and Abel's sheep were furnished by God through his benevolence and the fertility of his creation. Farming and herding both were a partnership between God and humans, with humans taking care of the creatures and God bringing the fertility. So the means of securing forgiveness through burnt offerings was still being conducted by God through his provision of growth to the land, crops, and herds.

God's covenant of life and fellowship which he had put in place in Eden is still in effect. Human sin and the fall necessitated some modifications to the covenant, but God did not abrogate it. God is still promulgating life and equipping humanity through the natural processes of creation, and he is still an interested God. His creatures are as fertile outside Eden as they had been inside of it. Fallen humans can still be God's people, they can still worship in God's indirect presence, and they can still receive God's redemption through substitutionary atonement in sacrifice.

As an early human navigating the new terrain after the fall, Cain could make ritualistic sacrifices. We are not told what caused Cain's sacrifice to be rejected. The typical answer that it was Cain's bad attitude has some merit given his later actions, but it is still a guess and not a rock-solid answer from the Bible. Another frequent suggestion is that Cain's sacrifice was rejected because it was not one involving blood. This argument doesn't work, though, because in Leviticus 2 there is a series of laws about cereal offerings in which grains are commanded as sacrifices. Many crop products are acceptable sacrifices, and none have blood. Why does the Bible not give an explanation for Cain's unaccepted sacrifice? The story is not concerned with the reason for the rejection of the sacrifice, but with Cain's response to that rejection. No reason is given for the LORD's veto of Cain's sacrifice, and there is not even a hint that there is an ostensible reason. It seems to be an arbitrary act on God's part. The text focuses on Cain's reaction to the behavior and authority of God, over which Cain had no control. God's statement to Cain holds out the opportunity that even though Cain could not make his *offering* be accepted, the right response to God's act would make *Cain himself* acceptable. God frequently puts us in or allows us into situations over which we have no control. If we respond well, we too will be acceptable. God doesn't demand that we be in control; he demands that we obey and love him in all circumstances.

The story of Cain continues the pattern of covenant, sin, and redemption which we saw in the creation story. After the resurgence of hope beginning under a new covenant of life with babies being born and crops and herds growing as God is watching on, Cain decides to disobey. Death is again the result of that defiance. Cain takes after his parents and after murdering his brother tries to hide his sin, but also like his parents, he finds that God wins that game. God sees sin and is aware of the killing. Our best efforts to conceal our sin are about as effective as the three-year-old's insistence that she didn't get into the candy, even while frantically trying to wipe chocolate off of her face. God is quite knowledgeable about our particular sins and of all of them. He knew Cain's sin in spite of Cain's denials. God also judged Cain's sin and punished it appropriately.

Once again, God's actions had made things good. Human sin tarnished and even demolished some of that goodness. But like the Eden story, sin and death aren't the final word. Sin isn't the end of the matter. Cain recognizes that his sin makes him deserving of banishment and death and that God deals with sin. But God also is willing to forgive sin and provide forgiveness. His mercy and grace prevent Cain's immediate death. He is given a mark of God's protection and goes on to have a family and a life.

Cain was protected from death by God's forgiveness, but not from the fractured family relationship. Sin has entered the arena, and many of the ramifications of sin are permanent. Sin once again brought death. But the last word is still God's love and grace.

Covenant

In our readings of the stories of Genesis, we have seen that the concept of covenant is strongly present, even if implied more than stated. With Abram, that changes and a clear, formal, verbalized promise between Abram and God takes center stage. This covenant will go on through Abram's descendants as God's covenant with Israel, the chosen people. It will appear in several subsequent iterations: Bethel/Jacob; Sinai; Zion/David; Josiah/Deuteronomy. All are direct continuations, developments, and restatements of the original covenant between God and Abram, and all contain the same four basic elements which we will see in Genesis 12.

The word (ברית *beriyt* or *covenant*) is a fancy term with a less fancy meaning. As was said before, this Hebrew word could equally well be translated as *treaty, contract, bargain, deal,* or *agreement.* So it would be accurate to say that God and Israel had a contract, or that they had a deal, but it doesn't sound very pious that way, so we will stick with the word covenant.

The account of the original covenant between God and Abram is found in Genesis 12. The first element we see in the covenant is a command from God: "Go. . .to a land I will show you" (verse 1). This command is specific to Abram alone, but it sets up the idea that in the covenant God is in charge. God is creator and

LORD; Abram is created being and subject. But remember that we saw in Genesis 1–3 that God's commandments are life and blessing. The tree of knowledge of good and evil was forbidden in order to prevent death and suffering. All of God's orders bring goodness, and obedience avoids a lot of unpleasantness.

The commandment in this version of the covenant is quite simple and short: "Go." It is also imprecise, lacking a defined destination. It is merely noted as "the land that I will show you." Subsequent versions of the covenant are less nebulous and more detailed in their directives, but all of the covenant agreements require a similar level of faith and a great level of commitment on the part of the chosen people. All versions of the covenant promise life and blessing as well.

These bestowals of life and blessing are explicit in the second element of covenant in which God makes a promise to Abram: "I will bless you" (verse 2). This gift from God is much more than a quick blessing at the end of church service or a perfunctory blessing over food. The goodwill laid on Abram was not simply pious good wishes—it was a concrete, physical bestowal of a gift consisting of health, wealth, and well-being for the future. In a sense God is promising to make Abram prosperous. God's statement also entails spiritual blessings, but it equally means physical abundance, including possessions. It also specifically included offspring numerous and great enough to possess a land and become a nation (verse 2).

The blessing was not limited to Abram and his family but extended to "all the families of the earth." In other words, Abram would benefit greatly by the covenant, and through him the blessing would be offered to all humanity. This is similar to the concept in Exodus 19:6 where Israel is said by God to be "a kingdom of priests." Priests mediated God to humanity, and Israel would be the medium through which God would reveal himself to the world, a process which began with Abram's obedience and attentiveness to God. Then Christ came to earth as an Israelite, one of the descendants of Abram promised in this passage, who extended salvation to everyone, thus fulfilling the covenant.

"So Abram went" (verse 4). He obeyed God. This is the third element of the covenant: obedience. Abram didn't give intellectual assent to a theological concept. He didn't mentally follow the Romans' Road. He didn't accept five points of anything. He didn't "like" it on Facebook. He packed up his stuff, gathered his people, and travelled down a dusty, muddy, rutted physical road toward an unknown destination. He performed works. In summary, he obeyed. Here we see belief and faith, certainly, but we see it by Abram's actions, by his literal following of a firm command, which is the third element of the covenant. Abram showed his faith by his actions, just like James says to do (James 2:18). He believed God's promise, and he did what it took to secure it. Abram didn't just think affirmatively about God's expectation and reward; he took real action to follow and receive. While Abram had a great degree of faith and belief, it was manifested in doing and in obedience to God's command.

The lack of clarity in the instruction to go emphasizes the spiritual confidence and devotion which are required by Abram and Sarai in following out the commandment. It requires that they trust God's guidance without relying on their own ideas. But to go calls for at least a spatial direction. Abram simply resumes his former journey in which his family's goal was Canaan (11:31) but which for some reason was terminated in Haran. God required a great degree of faith from Abram in sending him to an unforeseen spot, but Abram still used his best judgment to think of the most realistic way to go about all this. There had been some reason for Terah to set out for Canaan, and Abram apparently continued the original journey. God required faith but not impracticality.

In this same vein, Abram and Sarah act prudently by taking several people and all their belongings with them, which strongly implies a significant level of planning and preparation. Again,

Abram and Sarai set forth on faith but still make the most practical decisions. More people equaled more protection and more workers. More possessions make them better supplied with objects to help them carry out life's daily tasks and able to weather rough spells long term. They show confidence in God, but they also show earthly prudence and wisdom, which God also expects of his people.

Abram travelled to Canaan where he stopped for a while at the town of Shechem (verse 6), where there was a widely known holy place with an oak tree as part of the sanctuary.[15] In response, God appeared to Abram and reiterated the promise. Abram responded to God's approach by building an altar to be used for sacrifice. In this we see the fourth element of the covenant: God's presence in Israel's worship.

In summary, God commanded Abram, blessed him with security and prosperity, and in return Abram followed instructions. God was there with Abram in the act of worship performed by his servant. Then, the covenant was complete, in effect, and Abram is off to a great start, but. . .

We've been seeing covenant, sin, and redemption as key parts of the Old Testament, and Genesis 12 is a great example of all three. We have just seen the basic covenant between God and Abraham which was enacted in Genesis 12:1–9. The second key part, sin, shows up in the rest of the chapter. Abram and Sarah got off on the right foot, listening to God, going to Canaan, and worshiping, trusting in the promise of blessing. Then they go to Egypt and mess it up hugely.

Abram is worried that if the Egyptians know he is the husband of the beautiful Sarah that they will kill him in order to possess her. So as a precaution, the couple pass themselves off as brother and sister, and not as a married couple. Her beauty attracts Pharaoh, who takes her into his harem, where he likes

---

15. Shechem was also a temple in later Israel, but it seems to have been a Canaanite holy place before it was an Israelite holy place.

her performance as his wife enough to reward Abram very handsomely. So think about it for a moment: that is not a good thing! Effectively, Abram is selling his wife's sexual services. That is certainly *not* in keeping with being obedient to God. This is definitely an example of sin following covenant. And we see another aspect of God's work within covenant, sin, and redemption wherein God sees sin, judges it, and acts. Pharaoh's house has some unspecified but severe troubles as a result. But think again for a minute. Here we see that the consequences of sin are not limited to the sinner. Had Pharaoh committed sin? No. He had acted quite honorably throughout the story. He made Sarah an official, legal wife, treated her as such, and honored his marriage covenant with her. She was probably a very junior wife with several more senior wives ahead of her in rank, but she was a legitimate wife.[16] Pharaoh is the good guy of the story, behaving thoroughly honestly and virtuously. When he found out the truth, he restored Sarah to her rightful husband, showing Abram's fears to have been groundless. Abram and Sarah are the not-so-good guys who, quite deservedly, get deported.

A main problem here is that Sarah, as a wife of Pharaoh, is expected to bear Pharaoh's children. If so, then her children are not the offspring of the promise, and therefore the whole premise of blessing and covenant is in grave danger. So God is true to his part in the covenant even though Abraham and Sarah aren't. God takes action to protect Abram and Sarah and sets things right. God through Pharaoh even allows Abram to retain his illgotten gains of livestock and servants received from his nefarious actions. So God blessed and protected Abram, keeping his part of the covenant even when Abram had not kept his. Here is a key point in covenant, sin, and redemption: God is faithful,

---

16. Part of every Pharaoh's job was to have a lot of children, so he had to keep several women pregnant. Rameses II had nearly 200 children. One wife couldn't handle that, so he had a lot of wives, but they were wives, not mistresses, legal spouses bearing legitimate children.

even when Israel is not. Abram broke the covenant, freeing God from being bound by it, but God acted as though the covenant were still binding.

God offers redemption to sinful Abram and Sarah. Justice would have required the abrogation of the covenant and Abram's loss of his blessing and promise. But with God's redemption, the natural penalty is voided and Abram is blessed as though the sin had not happened. The treatment was not earned by Abram and Sarah, but God provided it anyway. Again, this came at a price, and the cost was paid by an innocent victim. The wealth that Abram received in Egypt was a cost that was borne by Pharaoh, whose household was afflicted and who lost his bride gift for Sarah, even though he was blameless of sin and wrongdoing in this case.

In this chapter we have seen a very straightforward display of the Biblical themes of covenant, sin, and redemption. God offered a covenant like with Adam and Eve, and Abram worshiped in the presence of God. Then Abram violated the deal grievously. God reacted with seriousness. But God was consistent with the covenant even when Abram wasn't. God freely orchestrated release from sin in the form of liberation from an untenable situation. Even more, God generously allowed Abram to retain the wealth he had gained in Egypt. The LORD has shown his faithfulness once again.

Sacrifice of Isaac

This story leaves me feeling really unhappy—in a lot of ways. I'm really uncomfortable with God in this story. And uncomfortable is not really the right word. To be honest, I don't like him very much at this point. To make Abraham and Sarah wait so long for the promised son, then to give them that son and divulge that he's going to take him away—in a really frightful way—I can't at all understand why God would do such a thing. We are told to put our faith in God, but this story doesn't make me want to trust him. It makes me want to hide from him. I know that God demands much of us and that we are supposed to trust him and his will and he will bear us through every burden, yet I still am very unhappy with God asking this sort of thing and making Abraham go through such agony.

Even more, I'm uncomfortable with myself because of this story too. The main reason is that I know I couldn't pass the test God set for Abraham. I don't know if it's lack of faith or misplaced priorities or what, but I know I'd fail that one. I couldn't give one of my sons or grandchildren like that. Oh, I could give one to God, even in a sort of sacrificial way in that I might never see them again as long as they lived. For instance, if God calls one of them to go to some far-off place where I'll never have contact with them again, I could support that. I wouldn't like it, and I might even argue with God and pout about it a while, but I could do it. I could even accept the death of one of them in God's service or in a war. I really wouldn't like that, and I'd never get over it, and I'd be mad at God for a long, long time, but I could do it. But to simply give one of them over to imminent death, to watch them die, knowing I could stop it if I decided to—that is a test I couldn't pass. If that means that I love my children more than I love God, well, I don't like that either, but maybe it's true.

That's a major reason why this text leaves me unhappy. It shows a big weakness in my Christian life. It shows my faith as insufficient, less than Abraham's, and at the conclusion I don't like me very much either. So at the end of the story, here I stand, unhappy with God, unhappy with myself, and not liking God, not liking myself.

Maybe I should have picked a different story, huh?

No, this story has some important things to teach us, and they're some lessons that are hard to understand, hard to learn, and even harder to accept. A famous Biblical scholar, F. F. Bruce, once wrote a book called *The Hard Sayings of Jesus Christ*. One of these hard sayings was Luke 14:26: "If any one comes to me and does not hate his own father and mother and wife and children and brothers and sisters, yes, and even his own life, he cannot be my disciple." That is definitely a difficult saying, isn't it? That one and Matthew 10:34: "Do not think that I have come to bring peace on earth; I have not come to bring peace, but a sword." Both of those bother me. That's all right—they're supposed to bother us. Genesis 22 and the sayings by Jesus telling us that one of the requirements of being a disciple is to hate your own family show us that God demands a lot of his people, sometimes things that are hard and unpleasant. Things that bother us.

Being a follower of Christ is not for sissies and weaklings. It takes a real toughie to obey God's commandments. Jesus tells us that a Christian must deny himself, or as Christian theology puts it "die to self," and Genesis 22 gives us a good close look at part of what it means to deny ourselves. And it's a hard, hard lesson and a hard, hard test, one I know I can't pass. But God is very clear on this: we are supposed to put God absolutely first in our lives. Nothing is supposed to prevent us from living the fact that God *must* be more important than *anything* else. I certainly hope and pray that I'm never put to the test, and so far it doesn't look likely — but then Abraham would have said that it wasn't likely for him before the events in Genesis 22.

Let's not forget that God has put people to such a test, and unlike the test he gave Abraham, God carried it through for some people. One rather famous instance of that is in II Maccabees 7, when God's people were suffering a great persecution, one lady who maintained her public worship in the face of death was arrested with all of her sons. She and her boys were given the choice of denying God or being tortured to death. One by one, the sons refused to renounce their God, and they were killed. Last of all the mother also refused.

So far, I've made the story and discipleship look pretty grim and awful, haven't I? But as always, that's not the whole story. Like the Bible as a whole and the story of God's redemption, there's a happy ending to both the story of Abraham's sacrifice of Isaac and to God's requiring some hard things of us.

There was one more instance of a parent who faced the same test as Abraham, and like Abraham, this father passed. And this father passing the test shows why there is a happy ending to both stories.

The father in this story faced a choice somewhat like the mother we talked about earlier. There were some people who had committed a few crimes and were about to die for them. The father in the story faced a dilemma. He could either save the convicted criminals, who were guilty, in which case his son would die, or save his son and let the guilty people die. Some of you have already figured out which story this one is. If you haven't, it's the one we read on Good Friday, the crucifixion. God is the father in the story, the son who died is Jesus, and the guilty sinners are you and me and the people next to you and down the road. In short, all of us, all humanity. God faced exactly the situation I described earlier where he had to give his own son over to die. God could have stopped it; he could have kept it from happening. He didn't have to do it. But he did. Jesus died on that cross screaming out in torment to God his father who could have done something, but he didn't. God just let him die.

In an agony we'll never be able to imagine, God ignored his own son's cries, because to have answered him would have condemned us to an eternal hell of separation from God. That's a love we'll never be able to comprehend, that God loved us and sent his son. And while we were still sinners, Christ died for us. That truly is what love is. God's saved people will spend all eternity learning about and living in that love, and I'm not just talking about heaven. We're living in that love today. God's love and salvation are here right now. God faced the test. And because he loves you so much and so deeply, he did what we needed in order to be saved from our sin; it cost him his only son. I can't comprehend why he did it or how or why he loves us guilty sinners so much, but I'm glad he does. I'm glad it was God who faced the choice instead of me because I know I would have failed. But I also don't understand why, after what God went through, anyone would refuse God's gift of salvation. You don't have to be ready. You don't have to feel like it. You don't have to get some things straightened out first. You don't have to promise never to sin again. You just have to believe it and accept it—it's that simple and that easy.

Abraham's story ties in very closely with the Old Testament theology of sacrifice we have seen. The wages of sin are death, but God's love for humans is expressed as grace allowing the death deserved by the human sinner to be diverted onto a sinless substitute. The sacrifice of a sheep is the death necessitated by sin, but the penalty is suffered by the innocent sacrificial victim.

Animal sacrifice was incomplete and required repetition, however. This story would have spoken powerfully to the Israelite exiles in Babylon, who saw themselves very much in the position of Isaac in that the future existence of the chosen people was greatly endangered. God's provision of redemption for Isaac would have been a striking reminder that it was as certain for them as for Isaac.

Abraham's statement to Isaac that God will provide himself the lamb is showing that the true, perfect, complete, and final sacrifice must be furnished as the Son, Jesus Christ. So in this way we see the themes of covenant, sin, and redemption. First, Abraham's covenant with God requires his obedience to God. Second, the sins of Abraham, which do not appear here in the story but take place elsewhere (see the chapter on Genesis 12), necessitate death. And third, the redemption is the provision of the sheep to sacrifice in place of Isaac. These events imply prophecy of the ultimate sacrifice provided by God himself with the Messiah.

Another interesting link between Isaac and Jesus is that Isaac carried the wood for his own sacrifice, similar to Jesus carrying his own cross to the place of execution (John 19:17), although some commentators believe this not to be a legitimate comparison.[17]

A major critical question regarding this passage regards the place of the story and the history of the tradition in the development of Israelite theology. An important idea regarding this is that the story serves as a prohibition of human sacrifice. While it surely fulfills that purpose, its current form certainly does much more than that. Seeing it simply as an interdict could cause the reader to miss the serious literary tension between God's promise to Abraham and the terrible task given to Abraham in the story. Whether it is a polemic against child sacrifice or a story

---

17. Sidney Greidanus, *Preaching Christ from the Old Testament* (Grand Rapids: Eerdmans, 1999), 307-308.

about Abraham's faith is irrelevant. There is no need to choose—it's both. Numerous commentators point out some inconsistencies between the two interpretations, but the inconsistencies are probably intrinsic to the subject matter and need no resolution.

Another critical idea with theological significance is the connection drawn by II Chronicles 3:1 which calls Jerusalem's temple by the name of Mount Moriah, which is the name of the hill on which Isaac was taken to be sacrificed. This connects the binding of Isaac with the sacrifices at the Jerusalem temple and makes the sacrifice of the ram one of the foundational acts on which the services of the temple are built—with David's sacrifice of the oxen on the threshing floor being the other. This passage is an instance of the critical questions about a passage being much less important and central than the theological ideas and literary points. Those points of covenant and redemption are major themes in this text in nearly all interpretations.

Ultimately, this story makes great demands on believers, primarily that we grant God first place in everything, above our own lives and even our family. That makes it one of the "hard sayings" of Genesis.

The Conquest of Shechem

This story of Israel's taking of the city of Shechem is an example of covenant and sin, but the redemption element recedes into the background. One of the unusual elements of this story is that nobody wins, at least not conclusively. The text is often seen as presenting relationships between two peoples portrayed as actions by individuals and is likely a reworked conquest narrative.[18] It seems to be one of a number of biblical texts which appear to assume continued Israelite occupation of the city of Shechem from the events in the story until the monarchy.[19] John Skinner in *Genesis: International Critical Commentary* tries valiantly to separate the story into component sources, and while he correctly points out some inconsistencies in the text which may well be due to the compiling of sources, his results are unconvincing.[20] Von Rad is probably correct when he says that "ultimate scientific clarification

18. John Skinner, *Genesis ICC*, 421.

19. Skinner, *Genesis*, 421. This view is supported by Joshua's worship service at Shechem after the events of Joshua 1-7. Shechem is never conquered but is a worship center anyway. It could be seen as being a Hebrew city at the time of the entry into the land of the Exodus tribes. Jacob also includes Shechem as property he bequeaths to Joseph in Gen. 48:22.

20. Skinner, *Genesis*, 417–418. Skinner's book is frequently described as "outdated," but by that standard, so is Gen.

is no longer possible."[21] There are doublets and even triplets in the current text, and von Rad is almost certainly correct in his pessimism about untangling the threads. The literary history of the text is unrecoverable from the present state of the material, and any earlier shape of the material as a conquest narrative, etiology, or other genre has been almost entirely subsumed under a story about a family. Two general tracks are possible. The story may reflect a historical event from the patriarchal era, or it could be based on conquest traditions from tribes which did not enter Egypt but secured a base by conquering Shechem, traditions which later accrued with the Jacob saga.

There is probably some connection between Genesis 34 and the place of Shechem in the book of Joshua. In Joshua, the Israelites have gatherings at Shechem without ever having been said to have conquered the city. This hints that Shechem was already a part of the Israelite coalition and Genesis 34 may have been a partial explanation of why. Such questions are probably unanswerable given the current state of the text. In its present form it concerns the actions of Jacob and his sons as individuals in response to a provocation by the Canaanite who was then in the land.

This story contains several biblical principles within the narrative. A familiar one we see is that sin has consequences. This lesson is found in most biblical narratives and is a major point of the garden of Eden, David's census, Achan's sin, Korah and Dathan's rebellion, and the whole Deuteronomic history as explained in Judges 2 and II Kings 17. A closely related assertion found in Genesis 34 is that the consequences of sin are not limited to the sinner but can spread far beyond that and hurt many innocent people as well. Sin makes very big and attractive promises, but it actually delivers pain, suffering, and death, and not always to the sinner alone.

---

21. Gerhard von Rad, *Genesis*; Old Testament Library (Philadelphia: Westminster Press, 1972), 330.

Shechem the son of Hamor who lived in the town of Shechem made an initial mistake—a big, bad one in a common category of sin—sexual sin. Another biblical principle which is applied here is that sin mars and destroys what is best. Sexuality is one of God's great gifts to humanity, but it is also a danger ground for developing serious human sins resulting in much sorrow and distress. All sin separates us from God, but in terms of earthly consequences, sexual sins seem to be worse and cause more problems than some other types. The rationalization "I'm not hurting anybody but myself" is certainly not true of sexual sins because they usually bring pain, trouble, and suffering to several people.

Shechem made a sizable mistake with Dinah in seducing or raping her, but he seemed to have tried to do right after that. Verse three says that Shechem loved Dinah. The verb *love* is used both as feeling the emotional attachment and also as recognizing a covenant relationship (e.g. Exodus 20:6; Deuteronomy 7:13; Malachi 1:2–3), so his offer may have been one of obligation as well as (or instead of) emotional love. If so it may indicate that Shechem saw his sin and tried to atone for it. His request to marry Dinah can be seen as being willing to make restitution as much as possible. What he offered was seen as good in Israel and was later enshrined in Israel's legal tradition and incorporated into the Torah (Deuteronomy 22:28–29).

While this offer of marriage could be seen as an honorable solution, there was a big problem: Shechem was outside of the covenant people and their close relatives. That Jacob and his immediate forebears saw this as highly significant is shown by Eliezer's trip to Haran to secure an appropriate wife for Isaac and Jacob's trip there to seek his own (Genesis 28:1–2).

This desire to maintain a separation from Canaanite society was probably a central point of the story to Israel. In the view of the writers, shapers, transmitters, and recipients of the traditions which comprised the Bible, Canaanites were idolaters and polytheists. One of the chief components of this was moral degeneracy as found especially in fertility rites connected with fertility worship. So for Israel to join itself to Canaanite society was to be joined to blasphemous behavior and the debauchery of sacred prostitution.[22]   Were Jacob to agree to the marriage of Dinah to Shechem, he would be approving of the terrible sin of Canaanite idol worship. Of course, the Bible is quite clear that Israel was a frequent and great offender in profaning the one true God. From the worship of the Moabite god Peor (Numbers 25:1–15), to Ezekiel's report of weeping for Tammuz (a Babylonian fertility god [Ezekiel 8:14]), to the women of Israel making cakes for the queen of heaven (Jeremiah 7:18), Israel seems to have been ever-ready to fall into Canaanite religion and practices. Even the temple in Jerusalem had to be cleansed of vessels holy to Baal and of the קדשים (*qodesim* or *sacred ones*), who were probably sacred prostitutes (II Kings 23). This constant attraction and temptation which fertility-oriented religion exerted on Israel resulted in orthodox Israel's vitriolic denunciation and condemnation of Canaanite religion, idol worship, and those who allowed themselves to be drawn into such activities. In this light, this story may well reflect the Israelite attitude seen in Joshua and the whole Deuteronomistic history that God intended Israel to exterminate the Canaanite pagans (Deuteronomy 20:16–18; Judges 2:1-5).

Such revulsion underlies the text's presentation of Jacob and his sons being so unwilling to join themselves with the city of Shechem, even though in purely economic and social terms it would have been an advantageous situation. But the religious and moral cost in the Israelites' eyes was much too high. So however honorable and honest Shechem's offer, it was unacceptable to Jacob and his sons. Thus, no simple solution was available to Jacob.

---

22. Ritual prostitution was apparently a regular aspect of the worship of Baal who was seen in Canaanite religion as the bringer of fertility and prosperity. Baal worship probably included worshipers having sex with the priests and priestesses as a means of inducing Baal to send prosperity. This practice was roundly condemned by the Levites and prophets.

His daughter had been badly wronged, calling for some response, but the proposed solution was completely unsatisfactory.

Shechem tried to solve the problem, but the whole bad situation stemmed from his initial sin and lack of self-control. Had he behaved himself, the whole crisis would not have arisen. The law of unintended consequences certainly applies to sin, as Shechem found out.

Dinah's role in the situation has been the focus of much speculation but cannot be known. Some commentators believe that Dinah may have intentionally been investigating the polytheistic Canaanite religious practices. While this is possible, there is nothing in the text to support such an idea. In fact, for all of her centrality to the events depicted, Dinah is not really a character in the story, and we know nothing of her role in the events. She may have been gallivanting in forbidden territory and failed to keep separate from sin. Or, it has even been suggested that she went looking for trouble, but we can't know what the text doesn't tell us.

Jacob was in a tough position with no good courses of action available. His daughter Dinah had been badly wronged, and he had to respond in some manner. Shechem was making serious offer of restitution, which had to be considered and answered.

Jacob's sons wanted revenge instead of restitution. In their position this wasn't unreasonable. In that time and place, their only security was their own ability to protect themselves physically. The willingness to employ violence in defense of one's family and clan was the main form of protection to stateless groups like Jacob's family. But an analysis of the respective forces led Jacob and his sons to be cautious about direct action.

Deciding against direct military action at that moment, the brothers adopted a stratagem which would give them an advantage in the planned confrontation of the future. A surprise attack when the enemy is in reduced defensive readiness is always a good military tactic. The sons of Jacob made the demand that the male inhabitants of Shechem's city be circumcised, and this aimed at setting up that situation.

Levi and Simeon, Dinah's full brothers, took the lead in the eventual actual military action and apparently did the actual killing, but all of their brothers participated in the looting of the city afterwards. Their hot-headed and rash violence was seen as excessive, even by Jacob. Even if protecting themselves was a good thing, they went overboard, and many people were killed or badly harmed who were not guilty of any wrongdoing.

This story shows that sin leads to more sin which expands exponentially to even more sin, and it all gets to be one giant mess. While covenant and sin are clearly present in this story, it is equally clear that there are no winners in this story, and redemption is generally lacking. Everybody loses something, and the only hints of saving grace are the restoration of Dinah to her family, the family's continuation, and the ill-gotten economic gain. Therefore, sin can be seen as the main lesson in our story. Sin makes enticing promises, but it always delivers negatives. The grandiose promises made by sin are actually big lies, and the gain is illusory and temporary. The price always outweighs the benefit, often greatly so. Too often, as in this case, everybody loses from sin.

The main loser in sin is God. God loved us and sent his son. With his stripes are we are healed. While we were yet sinners, Christ died for us.

Moses in the Bulrushes

The birth story of Moses, in addition to being a sign of the importance of Moses to Israel, contains some important theological themes. One is that God is present with Israel and is working to bring about the redemption of his people. Another theme is that God works on his own schedule. And as always there are many more subsidiary themes in the story.

The story begins by relating the marriage of Moses's parents and makes a point of establishing the Levite ancestry of both of them. Since Levi was the priestly tribe, and the priests acted as mediators between God and Israel, this lineage establishes Moses's credentials as the Levitical mediator of the covenant between God and Israel at Mt. Sinai. Priests took the sacrifice brought by the people and offered it to God and then pronounced God's forgiveness of sin to the repentant worshiper, thus mediating the worshiper's repentance and God's forgiveness.[23] Moses had priestly credentials to mediate the covenant in the same vein as the priests' credentials allowed them to mediate forgiveness.[24] This Levite background of Moses serves as a base for the whole

---

23. Ps. 20:4–5, 28:8–9, and 130:7–8 all seem to contain a priestly response pronouncing God's forgiveness to the worshiper.

24. Another type of Levite mediation is seen in Mal. 2:6 and Deut. 33:10 where Levites' preaching is presented as mediating God's word to Israel.

story of the exodus. All the events are centered on a Levite who, though raised as a gentile, remains within the bounds of his heritage. A side issue in chapter 2 but of great significance later in Exodus is that this story also establishes the Levite standing of Moses's brother Aaron who will later be anointed as the high priest.

The story in chapter 2 certainly reflects our themes of covenant, sin and redemption. The whole story of Moses's early life is firmly rooted in the concept of covenant and shows how God is faithful to the pact, overcomes the sinful suppression of Israel, and begins the process of liberation. Egypt's oppression of Israel through forced labor and the slaughter of the Israelite babies is clearly sin. Redemption is evident in the rescue of Moses from Pharaoh's edict and, in a larger sense, in God's orchestration of the ongoing preservation of Moses's life so that he can one day be the liberator and lawgiver for his people.

Our story begins with an act of disobedience to the laws of Egypt. Normally the Bible encourages obedience to civil law, but it leaves room for exceptions, and this case clearly constitutes one of those. Obedience to civil authority is commanded by Paul and by Peter, but in both of those texts, obedience is tied to the authorities maintaining order and peace, which is not remotely the case in Exodus 2. Here the authority is definitely being used in opposition to God's law and is perpetrating a serious injustice. Moses's mother, Jochebed, is obeying a higher law. As a result, God works a great thing through her courageous steadfastness.

But Moses's family had to pay attention to practicality. They hid the baby for as long as possible, but when that hiding place was no longer a realistic possibility, they took the next best option, which was to conceal him somewhere else. Unlike depictions of this event in popular culture, Moses was not set adrift in the river current. He was put into the reeds which normally grow in marshy areas where the current is much less than in the river proper.[25] Also, his sister was able to watch the basket, which indicates that it was moving very slowly, if at all. So the family did not abandon Moses to the river but continued to watch over the baby.

In reality, the placing of the baby in a basket in the river marsh was less an attempt to hide him than an act of desperation. It was a last-ditch effort with the wild hope that something good would come of it. It was trying to turn the intended instrument of destruction into one of deliverance, a maneuver which through God's intervention was successful. God doesn't promise always to rescue us, especially when we act in ways that are contrary and perverse. In fact, he usually expects well considered, rational decisions from us. But he certainly sometimes uses such abnormal, inscrutable acts and even requires them of his people at times, such as at Jericho, where Joshua's tactics would not pass muster at any military training school. Jochebed was certainly in a situation where the saying "Extreme times call for extreme measures" applied. And God was in it to work his plan. When Jochebed and the sister did their best for God, God worked with it and accomplished his purpose.

In addition to working through such strange acts as the basket in the reeds, God was also at work in routine, mundane acts such as bathing. The Egyptian ladies came to the river for their own reasons, but God had an additional purpose for their trip there. It was not chance that made the ladies and the basket come to the same place in the river at the same time. It may have been because the Hebrew women knew where the royal court normally bathed, but if so it was God again working through normal, rational decisions.

---

25. There is frequent, valid comparison of Moses's story to that of Sargon of Akkad, but the reedy marsh points to a major difference: Moses was not abandoned by being set adrift on the river, but hidden on it, still under the watchful care of his family.

The Egyptian princess saw the basket, was curious, and saw a baby inside. Her response was to feel pity—compassion for the boy—but the Hebrew word חמל (*hml* or *had compassion*) also implies the idea of sparing the child.[26] She apparently knew the law, and she certainly recognized the baby as a Hebrew, but her sympathy was a higher priority for her than the law. Despite having recognized the boy as a Hebrew, she spared him and took responsibility for him.

God's tendency to use elements and conditions that are opposed to him to accomplish his purposes was seen clearly in the creation story, and we witness the same thing here. The Nile River, which was to be the instrument of baby Moses's destruction, instead became the means of his deliverance. Paradoxically, the royal family that issued the order for his death also took him from the river and maintained his life. God had again thwarted Pharaoh's attempt to destroy the chosen people, this time using a member of Pharaoh's own household. It is in a sense a contest between two divinities: Yahweh the God of Israel versus Pharaoh and the Nile, both of whom in this latter pair were seen as divine by Egyptian religion. Of course Yahweh comes out the clear winner. Both God and Pharaoh had a plan for Moses, but only God's plan was accomplished. Pharaoh's scheme for Moses is stymied by his own family, yet God's design is accomplished through the faith, love, and obedient actions of a mother and the pity of a daughter. In the process, the daughter becomes a foster mother.

The sister's response to Moses's rescue by the princess again shows that Moses's Hebrew family did not abandon him to the river but maintained watch over him. Nor did they simply leave it all up to God. The sister kept watch over the basket and when an opportunity presented itself, she jumped in to affect events. And God used her efforts to bring about deliverance, both of Moses

---

26. Francis Brown, Charles Driver, Charles Briggs, *Hebrew and English Lexicon of the Old Testament* (Oxford: Clarendon Press, 1951), 328.

and eventually of Israel. God is always at work on a long-range plan.

In pursuit of that project, God is hard at work in the lives of his people, and he is faithful to his covenant. Even when things seem to be going terribly wrong, God is present and engaged. God's business in Exodus 2 is like a rope running through all of the elements of the story, tying it all together, linking and guiding. God himself is not a major character and is not even mentioned directly in the text. Nothing is attributed to his direct intervention, but his work with his people leading to the accomplishing of his will is the major theme of the story. God is committed to his covenant with Israel, overcoming sin and opposition to bring redemption to his faithful people. God turns his opponents' devices to God's own purpose as seen when he used the Nile and the royal family to deliver Moses. God is always at work, even when his part in the events isn't visible.

Worship on Sinai

This story contains one account of the worship ceremony sealing the covenant between God and Israel which has been in prospect since chapter 19. It is also, of course, an integral part of a larger block of material regarding the stay at Mount Sinai and the enactment of the covenant.

Israel is encamped at Mount Sinai and has agreed to accept God's offer of covenant (19:8). God has given the Ten Commandments (20:1–17) and the body of law known as the Covenant Code (20:21–23:33), which is probably from one of the northern tribes and quite different from Jerusalem's priestly concept of law.

While the chapter is most likely a composite, it has been edited with a coherent theological purpose in mind. Childs says that the composition history of Exodus 24 has "called forth a great divergence of opinion" with the only general consensuses being that verses 15b–18a only are from the P source, and that verses 1–2 and 9–11 form a different unit into which verses 3–8 have been inserted. Childs points out the difficulties in assigning the latter two sections to J or E and calls that kind of labelling undependable. Childs says, "The arbitrariness of much of this reasoning does not increase confidence" and that "the evidence is no longer such as to permit this detailed reconstruction." As we have seen in this study, attention must be paid to the final form of the text, and while source analysis can be a helpful tool in interpretation, it must not be used as a replacement for the canonical reading.

So in this case we will move straight to the interpretation of the finished text.

The first step in the covenant ceremony is God's invitation to Moses, the priests, and the elders to "come up to the LORD." Here Moses and company are summoned to approach God's presence. God is exalted and holy, but humans, who are neither exalted nor holy, are invited by God to come near to him. God then comes near *to us* as we see in God's descent to Mount Sinai in order to effect the covenant with Israel. Prophet (Moses), priest (Aaron and sons), and ruler (elders)—all classes and types, none excluded—are welcomed up to be part of the ceremony. Even the regular people are summoned, although to remain at a distance, at the foot of the mountain.

One of the main purposes of the invitation which God extends to Israel is worship. This story gives an account of the forging of the covenant which is enacted at a worship service. Israel is requested to draw close to God, and the main way of approaching God is through celebrating him—in this case formal, ritualized, programmed worship. So Israel's first step in that covenant relationship is showing God adulation. Worship brings Israel into God's presence and changes them into God's people. Like Israel, the church is invited and commanded to worship; it is both a privilege and a duty, not an optional possibility. In divine services we are brought before God and made over into his people.

Israel is drawn into God's presence in veneration, but God's holiness must be respected and not transgressed. While the people at the base of the mountain and the non-ordained elders play a crucial part in the ceremony, worshipping from afar, Moses the Levite and Aaron the priest play a leading role too. In Israel, priests were mediators who represented the people to God and God to the people. As a result only the priests could enter the temple inner courtyard, only priests on duty could enter the temple building, and only the high priest could enter the holy of holies.

Israel is to worship afar off at the foot of the mountain while Aaron, his sons, and the elders go up the mountain, but only Moses is told to approach the LORD directly. In this arrangement we can see Israel's concept of a hierarchy of worship. All Israel worshiped in the outer temple courtyard, the priests alone entered the inner court, only priests with specific functions and on duty entered the temple proper, and only the high priest entered the holy of holies. But in this story only Moses is told to approach the LORD directly. Of course, Moses is not the high priest since that office was given to Aaron, but Moses's role as the mediator of the covenant apparently gives him priestly rank above even Aaron, at least at this initial covenant ceremony. One element of the theology of this hierarchy is rather straightforward: all Israel is able to approach God in worship and enter the sacred precincts, but to go closer is limited to ordained personnel. God's holiness and presence must be recognized, respected, and not trespassed upon, but no one is shut out of experiencing them.

The seventy-four men who ascended the mountain that day are said to have seen God in terms that John seems to have borrowed for Revelation. The plain view of God was not limited to ordained priests and Levites but included the seventy lay elders. The lay Israelites, though, as said, were unable to closely approach the holiest place and required a go-between in the person of the priests. The sin of the common people separated them from God so that they could not directly approach him; therefore, they required a mediator (Exodus 20:18–20). Moses, Aaron, and Levites were partial and temporary intercessors, but Christ is the perfect eternal intermediary on our behalf (Hebrews 9:15, 24; I John 2:1). With Christ's death, the veil separating God's presence in the holy of holies from humanity was torn in two, enabling access to the Father for all humanity without the ministrations of a human priest. So all believers are now priests who can go directly to God.

In this Old Testament sequence, the presence of Nadab and Abihu are noticeable. Their inclusion in the instructions and in the party ascending the mountain is of intense interest to those attempting to trace the history of the belief tradition and the composition history of the Pentateuch. Scholars have formulated particular theories to answer questions they have about Nadab and Abihu being there. But those lines of thinking have minimal impact on the understanding of the text theologically. In the finished Exodus 24, these two men represent the Aaronide hereditary priesthood. They are Aaron's sons and priests as well. Nadab and Abihu die for their sin soon after, but they are remembered as important people, because they attended the mountain service.

In verse four we hear of the construction of an altar and the erecting of pillars at the foot of the mountain. Altars and pillars were standard artifacts of Israel's worship and were normal appurtenances of holy places (Genesis 12:7–8; 28:18; 35:3; I Samuel 7:12; I Kings 7:15–22). Here we see Moses and Israel engaged in official, conventional worship at a holy place with pillars. Exodus 19 states that God's presence on the mountain renders it holy then, and the altar and pillars built by Moses and Israel permanently mark the holiness of the spot, and mark the coming of God in that place. Jacob in Genesis 28 and Samuel in I Samuel 7 both erect pillars to designate a holy place. Abraham constructs altars at Shechem and Bethel in Genesis 12 in response to God's appearing. Establishing pillars and altars commemorates a reciprocal connection between worship and the presence of God. Psalm 22:3 says that God "inhabits the praise of his people." This suggests that praise and worship are conducted before the face of God because they are the appropriate responses to it (Genesis 12, 15, 28; Judges 2, 6, 13; II Sam 24). There are twelve pillars, specifically said to correspond to the twelve tribes, all of whom were there witnessing the covenant worship service, making it a public, formal, and corporate act. The whole community gathered as one to enter the presence of God, to praise him, and to enter into covenant with him.

The construction of the altar is very significant since altars are intended for the specific purpose of offering sacrifice, which is a central element of this covenant service and of Israelite worship in general. We have seen in Genesis 3 and also in Leviticus 1:4; 4:26, 31, and 35 that Israel did not view sacrifices as gifts to God but as the means of receiving atonement for sin. Psalm 50 states unambiguously, as was mentioned previously, that God has no use for dead animals. The blood of the sacrifice is only used for symbolic purposes. The spiritual benefit of sacrifice accrues to the worshiper in the form of forgiveness. It reaches both the worshiper and God in the form of a restored relationship previously broken by sin. The sinner deserves to die, but God's grace diverts the death onto a replacement, and the worshiper receives pardon. "Substitutionary atonement" is the name for this concept in theological jargon, and it is a good way to think about Israelite theology of sacrifice.

The blood of the sacrifice which is placed on the altar and then on the people is the seal of the efficacy of the animal's death, thereby reuniting God and sinful humans. The Bible tells us that "the blood is the life" (Deuteronomy 12:23), so when the blood is poured out of the sacrificial animal, the life is emptied as well. According to verse 6, the drained lifeblood is placed on God through the vehicle of the altar, representing the presence of the supernatural and insubstantial God. According to verse 8, then the drained blood is put also on Israel, reestablishing the broken connection between creator and created. The death absorbs the sins of the worshiper and brings about reparation of the relationship which had been crumpled by sin.

Not only the blood but the flesh of the sacrifice connects God and worshiper. Just as the blood is placed on the altar and on the congregation, the flesh of the sacrifice is similarly split between being burned on the altar and eaten by the worshiper (verse 11; I Samuel 1:4; 9:23–24). This set of concepts is a very useful presentation of the Israelite theology of sacrifice. The Israelites have committed sins and are unable to make themselves righteous. Since "the wages of sin is death," the death of the Israelites would be the just result of their sin. But God loves his people enough that he extends grace to them; he makes it possible for the death they earned to be forestalled. The life in the animal's blood and tissue touches God and the people, reuniting the people and God. We see this theology again in Isaiah 6:67 where the angel takes a coal from the altar and touches Isaiah's lips, taking away the guilt and bringing about forgiveness. The demise of the animal which was burned has ushered in redemption.

The eating is also significant. Eating together is a social event as well as a nutritional exercise. Throughout the Bible the sharing of food is a symbolic extension of hospitality and protection as well as sustenance. In Genesis 14, Melchizedek brings bread and wine with which to bless Abraham and the Most High God. In Exodus, the Passover bread and lamb are seen as essentials of a solemn worship service. In II Kings 4:8 Elisha is given bread by the lady as a means of supporting his prophetic office. In Psalm 23 the psalmist speaks of the LORD preparing a table for him in the presence of his enemies, thus taking the psalmist under the LORD's protection. In the New Testament, the Eucharist is a powerful way of sharing food as a religious ritual establishing or strengthening the bond between those partaking of the elements. Luke 24 is especially clear that Jesus became known through the sharing of food at Emmaus. Acts 2:42 states that enjoying meals together, in fact, was one of the main activities of the early church in Jerusalem. So, getting back to the story in this light, the elders, Moses, and Aaron eating and drinking in the presence of the LORD confirms the close covenant relationship between God and the people of Israel, with Israel being represented by the men at the meal. God has indeed prepared a table before them and has joined them at the table symbolically.

There is a very significant theological point in the order of events in this blood and sacrifice story. The blood binds God and Israel, but in the middle of the ceremony is the reading of the book of the covenant. This combination of covenant ceremony including sacrifice and the reading of the law is a common idea in the Bible. Similar to verses 3–8, a sequence in Deuteronomy 27 has such a service commanded. In II Kings 23 Josiah leads all the people in the reading of the law as an act of entering into the covenant. The covenant is centered on the reconciliation of God with sinful, fallen humanity—a covenant of love, mercy, and grace. Obedience to God's law and sincerity are central parts of the reconciliation. This concept is a biblical theme widely seen. Isaiah 1:10–20 states the idea very straightforwardly when God tells Israel that their solemn assemblies and blood sacrifices are an abomination to him unless they are accompanied by righteous behavior. Amos 5:21–24 is equally blunt: "I hate, I despise your feasts. . .your burnt offerings. . .but let justice roll down like waters and righteousness like an ever-flowing stream." I Samuel 15:22 says, "To obey is better than sacrifice."

The reading of the law points out that a major element in any worship service is fellowship with and communication from God. Much of worship language is addressed to God, but it is equally important to *listen* to God as well. This is accomplished institutionally through Scripture reading and preaching, and many traditions include quiet time in worship for listening for God to speak. In Exodus 24, God takes the institutional approach through the formal reading of the law as a part of the service. This shows very clearly that God talks to us. Moses "wrote all the words of the LORD," which he read to the people (c.f. Hebrews

1:1). God certainly has things to say, and he communicates his will to us.

We have a direct revelation of God in Scripture, which is unchanging, comprehensible, and, at least since the printing press, accessible and open. It is the word of God for the people of God. It is not all we need to know about everything, but it is the perfect testament by God of himself to his people. It must be interpreted, preached, and applied, and all of this must be done through the Holy Spirit. God speaks to us in other ways as well, but Scripture is primary.

His word includes rules: "Thou shalt. . ., thou shalt not. . ." They're non-negotiable, they're absolute, and they're wholesome maxims. Obeying God's commandments isn't losing freedom, it's establishing "guard rails" for the self to maintain true freedom (e.g. traffic laws, barriers around holes, rails on bridges—all of which prevent disaster). In this text, our themes of covenant, sin, and redemption take a modified form: covenant is obviously the primary theme, and really, the covenant *is* redemption. It's redemption from slavery, from rootlessness, and from anarchy, disaster, and the grave.

Israel's response to their hearing of the word of God is to say, "All that the LORD has spoken we will do, and we will be obedient." Sometimes we humans get it right, and this was one of those times. Unanimous agreement to follow and be respectful of God was Israel's answer to God's invitation. That was a very smart move and an excellent response to God's desire that they enter covenant. Chapter 19 is even better. There they make an identical response without having heard the details, in effect signing a blank contract. Their faith in God is absolute. They don't need to read the fine print, or even the large print. They offered an absolute commitment to God and to his will, his commandments. Go thou and do likewise.

The Golden Calf

In one sense, the golden calf stories in Exodus 32 and the connected story of Jeroboam's golden calves in I Kings 12 are rather simple and easily understood, at least at a superficial level. The main point is a practical application of the second commandment: "Thou shalt not make unto thee any graven images," lest the LORD thy God smack thee upside thy head. Aaron and Israel did so, and so did God. Calf images were graven images, so they are therefore prohibited and are seen in these texts as the equivalent of polytheism ("These are your gods. . ."). So keep the first two commandments, don't worship any gods other than the one true God, and don't make images of him. Violating these commandments makes bad things happen. End of story.

Well, no, not quite the whole story. While that approach isn't at all wrong, and the second commandment is certainly the main point of the stories in their present form, there's a lot more going on in the whole golden calf series than that, both in the reconstruction of the history of the texts and in the final biblical form.

First, let's take a look at a historical approach to the golden calf story in Exodus and its companion story in I Kings 12. While scholarly commentators are virtually unanimous that the text of Exodus 32 is composite, there is no consensus on the sources behind the text. Good examples of this uncertainty are seen in the conclusions of two of the major scholars, Noth and Hyatt, who come to radically different conclusions regarding the origins of the various strata in our text. Consulting additional scholars results in further confusion except to see that, so far, source criticism is inconclusive.[27]

But biblical scholarship has many useful insights into the golden calf story even without ascertaining its sources, however. In particular, there are some interesting and intriguing connections with other biblical texts. One point almost all commentators agree on is that there is some kind of connection between the two stories about golden bull images which were made by Aaron and Jeroboam. There is a triangular connection among Aaron, golden calves, and Bethel which is very indistinct, but definitely there (figure 1).

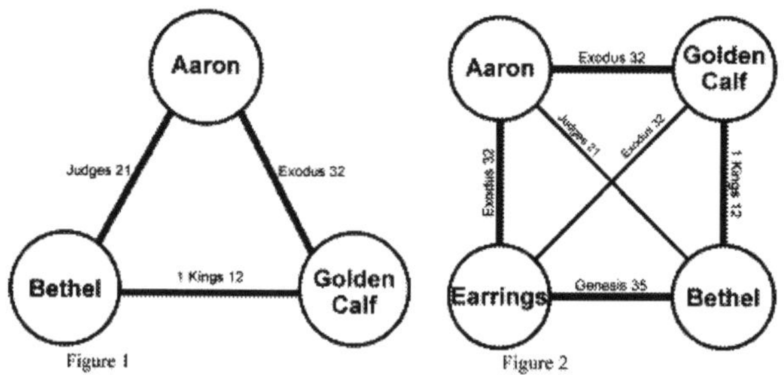

Earrings as seen in Genesis 35:1–4 also fit in here somewhere, again indistinctly (figure 2). In this story, Jacob and his family are going to Bethel, and as part of the preparation they take off their earrings. Jacob hides the jewelry under the oak tree and builds an altar. So we get earrings and Bethel connected. Judges 8:24–27 furthers the connection of pagan earrings being converted into Yahwistic artifacts by Gideon, even though the final editors of

---

27. Martin Noth, *Exodus* (Philadelphia: Westminster, 1962), 243–247; J. P. Hyatt, *Exodus* (Grand Rapids: Eerdmans, 1971), 301–304; Brevard Childs, *Exodus* (Philadelphia: Westminster, 1974), 557–558.

Judges inserted an anachronistic condemnation of the ephod of Gideon, which was probably perfectly legitimate in Gideon's day.

To give away the suspense, nobody knows what to make of this three-way (or four-way) connection. There is a lot of speculation, none of which can be tested for adequacy. But even though we don't have a conclusion, we can still examine the main factors to be considered.

One highly regarded theory is that Exodus 32 is a highly modified version of the Bethel priests' legend explaining the origin of the calf/bull at Bethel. The most probable reconstruction of the original version centers on Exodus 32:24 where the calf miraculously emerges from the fire when Aaron put the gold earrings of the people into the flames. The idea in verse 5 was probably a key element of the original legend and clearly connects the bull to Yahweh in both the hypothetical reconstruction of the original and in the Exodus 32 version. So in this view, the worshipers at Bethel had a cult legend in which the people gave their gold earrings which had polytheistic significance to Aaron, who put them into a fire, and Yahweh transformed the gold into the holy calf which then served as the emblem/seat/mount of Yahweh (who was thought to be invisibly present above the bull).[28] The bull represents characteristics of Yahweh: strength, protection, creative power.[29] In this hypothesized early form of the story, the bull as icon was directly instituted by Yahweh and an overt rejection of polytheism, having been fashioned from the destroyed gold earrings which were symbols of other gods, or at least of improper worship practices (Genesis 35:1–5; Judges 8:24–26; Num. 31:50). So Israel forsook other gods, and their earrings were transformed by God into a holy image in the shape of a bull. This is quite in keeping with standard Yahwistic theology: God transforms bad things into good. Remember, in Genesis 1 God

---

28. J. P. Hyatt, *Exodus* (Grand Rapids: Eerdmans, 1971), 301–309.

29. William Albright, *From the Stone Age to Christianity* (Baltimore: Johns Hopkins, 1940), 298.

converted the dark, primordial, chaotic deep into the good night and the ocean of creation. In Numbers 23, God turns Balaam's curses into blessings. God transformed death from the wages of sin into the means of receiving redemption. Closely related to this concept of sacrifice is the greatest example of God's turning bad into good, which is, of course, his altering of the crucifixion of Christ into the means of eternal salvation, thus converting sinners into children of the kingdom of God. In the whole story of the Exodus, God turns weak Aaron into the high priest.

In this hypothesis of the development of the golden calf story, Bethel was originally a legitimate temple but lost that status in the events related in II Kings 17, in which the Assyrians assisted the foreign colonists who had been forcibly resettled in Samaria. These foreigners converted the temple at Bethel into a shrine to Yahweh, but not one to Yahweh the *only* God, or even to Yahweh the *high* God, but to Yahweh the *local lion* god. That certainly was not legitimate Yahwism. Added to that is the probability that Bethel and Jerusalem had been perennial rivals and competitors for prestige even in the best of times. So we see that the stage is set for the Jerusalem folks who wrote the Deuteronomistic history to compose some really nasty accounts of the temple at Bethel. (But don't forget that those same orders of Jerusalem priests included in the Torah the story "Jacob's Ladder," which showed conclusively that Bethel was a very holy place.)

So the final editors of the Torah were highly opposed to worshiping Yahweh as a minor local lion god. They were also against worshiping any gods other than Yahweh. Sacrificial worship at any place other than the temple at Jerusalem was also prohibited. They also were against the use of images in worship, even if the images were used in regard to Yahweh as the only true God. None of this is any surprise. So why is the story of the golden calf made to reflect badly on Aaron, who otherwise was the founder, eponymous ancestor, and patron saint of the exilic and post-exilic Jerusalem priesthood? And why was Aaron granted redemption for establishing the calf but Jeroboam was not? These questions aren't directly answered in the text, and we can only make inferences.

My historical reconstruction of the origin and growth of the text is this: the Israelite Levitical priesthood at Bethel was associated with the name Aaron, and its holy symbol was a golden bull. Their cult legends included Jacob's ladder and the original story underlying Exodus 32. In this story as told in Bethel, Israel while at Horeb renounced polytheism and relinquished their gold earrings. These objects which had pagan associations were given to Aaron. He then put them in the fire where God miraculously formed them into the bull—a visible, physical sign and seat of God's presence with his people. Jeroboam gave royal support to this temple, priesthood, and cult legend. When images were later outlawed, and even later, when Bethel became profaned and desecrated by the Samaritans, it all came to be seen retrospectively as unwholesome. Then retroactively it was prohibited. Ultimately, the cult legend was transformed into a cautionary story against images of any sort (except for the cherubs in Jerusalem, of course) and, joined with an origin story about the Levite priesthood's covenant, was redacted into the book of Exodus in its current form. So we're left with some really intriguing possibilities regarding the connections and one actually very good possibility (the reconstructed Bethel cult legend of the bull image) but with no way to resolve them with any certainty. We're left with that initial understanding of the story as the only reliable one, the one where God says not to make any graven images and to worship him alone. It seems that sometimes a straightforward reading using the plain sense is the best reading.

This passage shows some of the limits of critical scholarship. Scholars can ask a lot more questions than we can answer, and this passage certainly fits that category. Critical scholarship has achieved some tremendous successes (the Documentary Hypothesis, the Deuteronomistic History, the Four-Source Theory, [and some overreaching ones (J1, J2, L, S, etc., Qa, Qb, etc.)]), but as we see in this study, it cannot replace a close examination of the clear meaning of the finished text. Critical study can be a valuable supplement to the clear (or unclear) intention of the text; however, it can never replace it.

So we will turn to an examination of the final version of the text as we find it now in Exodus. As we saw above, the passage is a practical case study of an application of the second commandment against making graven images, with a subsidiary theme against polytheism.

The first verse of the story both sets the scene for the account, states the general themes of the passage, and forms a summary of the sins as a whole. When Moses didn't reappear when they thought he should, Israel got impatient and tired of waiting on God to do something. In response, they substituted their own plan. This really is a very good definition of sin. Sin is prioritizing our own will before God's—essentially trying to be our own gods. This was seen clearly in Genesis 3 where the serpent tempted Adam and Eve with the idea that "you shall be like gods."

So Israel had made new gods, gods that they could control and carry around. In this way, the gods would always be where Israel wanted them to be and where Israel could see them. Isaiah 46:2 addresses this view of idols: "Bel bows down, Nebo stoops, their idols are on beasts and cattle; these things you carry are loaded as burdens on weary beasts. They stoop, they bow down together, they cannot save the burden, but themselves go into captivity." Handmade gods can be convenient, but they are useless, Isaiah says, since "they cannot save."

That is a characteristic of idolaters. They want to manipulate their gods and be in charge. This is similar to the story in I Samuel 4 where the Israelites misinterpreted the presence of the ark of the covenant as the presence and assistance of the LORD of Hosts. This was effectively treating the ark as an idol, and, as usual, the result of idolatry was disastrous.

Another problem seen in the first verse is impatience on the part of Israel. God took longer with Moses than the Israelites thought should have been necessary, so they decided to force things along according to their own schedule. Waiting is always hard, and waiting for God can be even harder. Being patient isn't easy, especially when we're in a hurry and God isn't. It's also difficult to tell when we're being impatient and when God is waiting on us to get started and do something.

In this case the uncertainty and impatience are a little bit understandable. The mountain is covered in smoke, fire, and lightning, and it was quaking. Then Moses goes up into all of that and isn't seen for six weeks. It's no big surprise that the Israelites wondered what had happened to him.

But Israel let its worry and agitation take its focus off of God. "This Moses, the man who brought us up out of the land of Egypt" is the subject of their anxiety instead of God, who really brought them out (cf. 33:1 where God says the same thing). Much of human sin includes such loss of focus on God, generally as a result of being preoccupied with ourselves instead.

The chapter exhibits a structure which manifests a series of contrasts which highlight faithfulness and faithlessness along with righteousness and sin. The first such binary opposition is seen in the holy and reverent gift of the God-inscribed tables of the law. These indicated God's trust placed in Moses on the mountaintop in contrast to the idolatry, revelry, and covenant-breaking at the foot of the mountain. As God delivers the law "Thou shalt not make unto thee any graven images," Israel is ironically busy doing just that. This is clearly a violation of both the commandment against graven images and the one to have no other gods. While *elohim* is used of God, the plural verbs in verse 1 (*make us gods, [they] who shall go before us*) strongly implies plural gods. Likewise, verse 4 shows multiple gods ("Behold your gods, . . .[they] who brought you out of Egypt"). This story tends to understate the accusation of polytheism, but the accusation is still clear in the plural verb. We saw above that the bull was originally seen as the pedestal of God, but in the final story, it replaces God, and the editors who put this text into its final form see the bull as a god. They take the same view as Isaiah 44 where the prophet makes fun of idols made out of wood from a tree which also supplies firewood for home heating and cooking. In our story, Israel is committing idolatry of the worst sort and committing polytheism, too.

A major problem with bull images, in Israel's view, was those images' close association with Canaanite polytheistic religion in which bull icons were common. We saw above how bulls represent characteristics of God, his creative power being one of those. The problem with that is that the bull's creative power is through sexual reproduction, which is much too close to Canaanite fertility rituals in which public sexual acts were thought to ensure productivity of soil, animals, and humans.

The fate of the image is also connected to Israel's views on idolatry. The image was burned and the ashes scattered on the water which Israel was forced to drink. In the desert, water is life, and their sinful image polluted their water. Idols contaminated Israel's life in the same way. Sin corrupts life, and its worst effects are focused on what is best about life. God provided water for Israel, but their idol contaminated it. A clear example of sin eroding what is best is seen in sexual behavior that involves moral dysfunction. Sex is one of God's great gifts to humanity, but sin has all too often made it the source of pain, degradation, disease, and misery.

Therefore, one can see that Israel's sin of idolatry and polytheism violated the first two commandments and was very nearly a mortal sin on the national level. All of the proliferating offshoots of sin from the animal image infected most aspects of life thoroughly. Yes, gold can certainly be tempting. Israel at least worshiped a golden *god*. Far too often, we simply worship gold.

Another sin Israel committed as associated with idolatry was the revelry. The festival started well but degenerated into pagan excess. In addition to the burnt offerings offered to the idol, Israel rose up to *play*. While this verb does not always entail sexual acts, it can be used for such as in Genesis 26:8; 39:17. In context of verse 6, it is not directly sexual, but a sexual connotation is not excluded. Given the pagan fertility connections of the bull image, it is probable that the final authors of the text intended to at least hint at sexual fertility rituals, in keeping with their tendency here to imply polytheism rather than making overt statements.

This wild pagan carousing contrasts clearly with the calm reverence of Moses atop the mountain in communion with God. This is not to say that physical behavior showing exhilaration can't be allowed. Several passages in the Bible clearly approve of loud, exciting musical worship that can raise the rafters. David even danced as part of worship as do Abyssinian Christian priests today. But such worship should not degenerate into excess, and the worship celebration must be celebrating God, not just celebrating.

Another strong contrast, though not entirely contained within the chapter, is the disconnect between the idolatry, polytheism, and revelry centered on the calf and Israel's earlier promise in 19:8 and Exodus 24:7: "All that the LORD has spoken, we will do." Alas, this unconditional commitment to God didn't last very long.

That underscores the overall problem in the Israelites' behavior, which was that they were violating the covenant they had already agreed to keep. Moses's breaking of the tablets of the law when he saw the calf is emblematic of the broken covenant between Israel and God. Moses shattered the tablets, but Israel had shattered the covenant even more thoroughly.

We see the behavior of Moses contrasted with that of Aaron, to Aaron's great disadvantage. Moses is the leader, taking charge and ending the worship of the calf and the pagan debauchery, while Aaron is the artisan who made the calf and generally led by the people. Aaron was not the leader of the people which God meant for him to be and instead was a weak follower, blindly led by them into terrible sin. Moses was the mediator of the covenant between God and his chosen people; instead, Aaron mediated an idol which aborted the covenant. Moses was the great law*giver*; Aaron was a great law*breaker*. Moses was faithful; Aaron was faithless. A contrast is also seen between Moses and the worst of the idolaters. The idol worshipers are unrepentant and persist in their sin. Moses intercedes for Israel, requesting God's mercy. Moses is irate with the people as is God, but Moses speaks up for Israel before God.[30]

Moses tries to deal with Aaron as well. Aaron was aware of his failure, since when confronted by Moses, he tried to make excuses and in verses 22–23 tried to blame the people for his own sin. Neither Moses nor God accepted the excuses, however. Just like God didn't accept the excuses of Adam and Eve in the garden, he wouldn't buy Aaron's attempts to shift blame, nor will he condone ours either.

Aaron is not without good qualities. In verse 5 he seems to try to keep the focus of worship on Yahweh, but his efforts are insufficient. His asking for gold earrings may be an attempt to eliminate the pagan associations as seen earlier, but even if so, he ended up simply exchanging one idol for another.

In the priestly realm, we see a major difference between the actions of Aaron and the work of the Levites. Aaron gave in to the pressure of the mob, became the sinner-in-chief, and was finally a failure in this event. The Levites, on the other hand, by being faithful to God were highly successful and showed tremendous zeal for the LORD, even at great personal cost. As a result,

----

30. A good statement of this leadership principle was made by former naval lieutenant Robert A. Heinlein. He said, "I'm tough as blazes on my (soldiers) myself. . .but if they're in trouble higher up, I've got to take care of my (soldiers)." Heinlein, *Tunnel in the Sky* (New York: Ace Books, 1955), 37.

they were given priestly rank and a special covenant with God, an eternal covenant, says Malachi in Malachi 2. This episode elevating the Levites in preference to Aaron probably stems from a period when the Levites and Aaronide priests were struggling for status in Israel; in this case, the story is obviously told from a Levite perspective.

We have been using the themes covenant, sin, and redemption as an interpretive tool, and this text certainly manifests those concepts very clearly. The issuance of the covenant is the background against which the entire Sinai section is played out. The covenant is straightforwardly outlined in the two tablets which Moses is given, with the commandments even written on them by God's own hand. Israel assents to the covenant, even before they know the stipulations (19:8); they had already been liberated from Egypt, which was one of the major promises of the covenant. The manna they ate every day was also a distinct blessing from their covenant. These aspects of the covenant are not mentioned directly in this story (except for the deliverance from Egypt), but to eliminate them would require taking the story completely out of its context, which wouldn't be right.

Israel's readiness to fall reminds me of the man who got married promising to be faithful every day but Tuesday, which in reality was a promise to be unfaithful. The golden calf established a pattern repeated throughout Israel's history in which this nation was all too ready to abandon the exclusive worship of the one true God to go "whoring after Baal," as the KJV puts it. Israel often went limping along of two opinions, as Elijah accused them.

We see the editors' evaluation of Israel in this part of the story. Unable to remain faithful to God, Israelites too often and too eagerly sought other gods, and the prophets and Levites castigated them sorely in the attempt to bring the nation back into the true worship of Yahweh, LORD of Hosts, God of Abraham, Isaac, and Jacob. A sub-theme under sin is that it brings God's judgment, and this story shows that markedly. Their water was polluted by the ashes of the calf, the Levites apparently killed about three thousand men, and an epidemic broke out among the people. Sin has consequences, and forgiveness and redemption do not necessarily entail the abolishing of them. In this case the price of the sin was quite severe, in keeping with the seriousness of the sin.

The theme of redemption is rather elusive in chapter 32 alone and consists primarily of the avoidance of annihilation. While that is a good thing, it is less than uplifting when seen in isolation. But it is a necessary precondition for the redemption which certainly comes in the larger cycle of which the golden calf story is a part.

An act of redemption which finds its fulfillment later is the elevation of Aaron to the high priesthood. God redeems the weak man who was led into idolatry and makes him into the great high priest who is faithful and who is the founder of the highest priestly family. Another pattern is manifested here. Aaron the spineless weasel is transformed by God's grace into a hero of the faith. Aaron was not selected as the high priest because of his qualifications. He was chosen by God, and then God qualified him for the priesthood. God gave Aaron the attributes which he needed to accomplish the task to which he was called.

In a similar way, the Levites were elevated to the priesthood and became great servants of God, but this time it was through their faithfulness. Being committed even in a very difficult situation opened an opportunity for even greater service.

The tent story in 33:7 may be the strongest presentation of redemption in the cycle since it clearly assumes the restoration of the presence of God in the camp, and all the people participate at a distance while Moses meets with God in the tent. In the arrangement of the texts, although God is not in the midst of the camp but on the periphery, he is there with Israel. This is apparently a reinstatement of the presence of God which was withdrawn in 33:3.

In addition to avoiding annihilation, Israel remained the chosen people, and the covenant remained in effect. As we saw with Abraham in Egypt, God is faithful, even when his people are not.

Hannah

In Judges 17 through I Samuel 3, Israel is at a low point. It is spiritually adrift and has fallen into apostasy, idolatry, and indifference. Even the highest priesthood has become infected with materialism, sexual misbehavior, and disrespect of God's laws and institutions. The Deuteronomistic history sees this cycle of sin and repentance as an important element in Israel's response to God's covenant with the nation.[31] The last chapters of Judges show how Israel had fallen into ritual error, mistreatment of people, and civil war. Any culture which finds itself in such a situation is one in decline, in trouble, and in serious danger of failing. All of this describes Israel at Samuel's birth, including the obviously impending fall of Israel to the

---

31. The Deuteronomistic history consists of Josh., Judg., I and II Sam., and I and II Kings. It is thought by some to have been completed by editing older materials into a connected treatise in two stages. The first rendition was probably completed during the reign of Josiah and was intended to support the reform enacted by him. A revision of that first draft was finished during the Babylonian exile and was intended to explain why Israel and Jerusalem were defeated. Martin Noth's *The Deuteronomistic History* is the classic presentation of this idea, with Frank M. Cross's *Canaanite Myth and Hebrew Epic* being a substantial revision of Noth's hypothesis. Richard Nelson in *The Double Redaction of the Deuteronomistic History, I & II Kings, Interpretation Commentary,* and in *The Historical Books* further develops the idea.

Philistines with the accompanying threat of the loss of cultural, religious, and national identity.

But, as we know, such a societal collapse and national fall did not happen to Israel. First Samuel 1–3 tells the beginning of the story of how the process was reversed. In this narrative, Elqanah was a farmer in Ephraim who went against the tides of the times. In an era of apostasy and idolatry, Elqanah persisted in the proper worship of the true deity at God's appointed sanctuary. He not only continued to worship, but he led his family in worship and brought the whole group to Shiloh to have them participate in religious observances. Even the children were part of the worship. They were only one family and far from perfect, but their faithfulness was used by God to accomplish great things. In this section of the story, we can see God's covenant at work again. Israel is living in the promised land, the land is producing enough to live reasonably well and to raise a family, and God is present with Israel in its worship at the holy places. The faithfulness of Elqanah shows the true acceptance and embodiment of the covenant in response to God's will.

As a result of Elqanah and Hannah's loyalty, obedience, and worship, the prophet Samuel was born and put into the situation where God wanted him and in which he could begin a great work for the LORD. However, in the locale of Shiloh, the temple didn't look like the best place to become a great follower of God. It was staffed by Eli's sons, who were committing terrible acts of greed and sexual immorality (and probably idolatry if, as is probable, the women at the door were ritual prostitutes of Baal). Sin had infected the highest house of worship in the land, and the priesthood itself was involved in the vilest of sins. Samuel would have been tempted to participate in these activities, but he took another way. While still quite young, Samuel was given a chance to hear the LORD speak, and though it took God three tries to get through, Samuel listened and obeyed. He thereafter became the great prophet who inaugurated the reign of the great

King David, through whom God brought about deliverance of Israel and through whose family God orchestrated salvation for all people.

Elqanah, Hannah, and Samuel certainly were tempted to give in to the pressures to participate in the sin and dissolution of the times, but in the final analysis when it counted, they stood firm for God against the trends of the times. Through their steadfastness, belief, and compliance, God brought deliverance and a reversal of the decline. As a result, Israel did not fall but prevailed. One person, one family standing firm for the truth of God, started the turnaround of the downfall by refusing to join the others in their fall into apostasy and began the return to greatness that was God's will.

The story does not get off to a promising start. Elqanah's family is prosperous and worships at Shiloh, but there is tension within the family caused by problems of childlessness and competition. Elqanah's remarkably insensitive response to Hannah's unhappiness couldn't have helped (verse 8).

This story has many similarities to the narratives in Genesis of Abraham, Isaac, and Jacob. In The Genesis stories about Abraham and Jacob, we see a man in a polygamous marriage, the wives in competition complicated by the childlessness of one of the women, the barrenness ended through God's actions, and the resulting son being the greatest of the children and the one through whom God fulfills a promise. Isaac's wife is initially barren and a younger son inherits.

Hannah's womb was closed by God's direct action, and she knew it. She was correctly blaming God for the problem, but her response to that problem and to God was badly off target when she refused to eat at Shiloh. The food she refused was a ceremonial meal consisting of the meat from the sacrifice, which was intended to effect atonement for sin. Not eating the sacrificial meal was refusing communion and rejecting the presence of God. Her rejection of the food was a reaction to God's action and a denial of the one who had closed her womb, which in most cases would be seen as a curse. Hannah was unhappy and not just at the dismal situation—she was mad at God.

Hannah didn't understand the cause of this circumstance; she didn't want to know why God had arranged things this way. She wanted children. She wanted God's blessing in a very tangible form: a baby. But in refusing to have the communion with God, she was turning away from the one who was the answer to her predicament. And the obvious and predictable result of that was years of bitter weeping.

But one year, something not noted in the text made Hannah change. That year, instead of crying and refusing to eat the sacrifice, Hannah made a radical turnabout and went to the temple and prayed. Instead of pushing God aside, she sought his presence. Instead of just being angry, she sought him at his place of worship and talked with him. And that action made all the difference. Hannah worshiping and praying in the presence of God brought about a very different situation than the one in which Hannah had been avoiding and rejecting God. By turning *to* God instead of *away* from him, Hannah entered a completely new dynamic in which he would work a tremendous transformation in her—not just in Hannah's attitude, but in her whole self, in her family, and ultimately in her nation, the chosen people. This turning to God which Hannah exhibited may not be classical repentance like that portrayed in theology textbooks. It is certainly real returning to God since we see this type of repentance under coercion also presented favorably in I Kings 8:47–48. Here, Solomon's prayer comments favorably on God's people repenting because they have been carried away into exile due to their sins. Also, Amos 4:6–11 gives a list of the punishments God set on Israel trying to induce repentance: "Yet you did not return to me." Yet more, Isaiah 1:6 states, "Why will you still be smitten, that you continue to rebel?" All of these make clear that God uses strong-arm tactics to bring people back to him, so Hannah's prayer under duress is acceptable to God. The subsequent birth of Samuel and his full brothers and sisters also attests to God's acceptance of Hannah's last-resort repentance.

Hannah's contrition was less an emotional change than an outward act. Her divergence from previous behavior was a conscious decision: she would act in faith and then hope that the faith in God would be successful. The turning to God and repentance was not so much an inward change as physical activity: she went to the temple and sought God's presence through prayer. We can see faith as an action instead of an emotion in other texts. In Mark 1:40–45, the leper acts by approaching Jesus, kneels, and asks to be made clean. In Mark 2:5, Jesus saw the faith of the men bringing the paralytic; he viewed their actions, not their feelings. In II Kings 5:14, Naaman washed in the Jordan and was healed in spite of his feelings, emotions, thoughts, and beliefs.

Hannah's encounter with the holy God happened in a holy place. The shrine at Shiloh was an important regional temple; like all high places of that nature, it was seen as a location where God was present in a special and direct way. Genesis 28 makes this point about Bethel, which was revealed to Jacob as the spot where the staircase from heaven touched the earth. Shechem in Genesis 12, Bohim in Judges 2, and Gideon's home village in Judges 6 are all examples of holy sites where God appeared in visible form. While Israel was aware that God was present everywhere, they saw him as being particularly present at holy places, and Shiloh was one of the holiest. It was there that Hannah tried to reconnect with God after rebuffing him for years, and her seeking after God began a major change.

Once she had sought God's presence, she worshiped. At that stage she probably wasn't feeling especially reverent or pious. In fact, she was still in great distress. Her worship seems to have consisted of bitter resentment more than impassioned praise, but she went through the motions anyway. Her worship wasn't full of gratitude, praise, or any other such exalted feelings, but it was still something positive. Her worship, like her faith, was an action, not a feeling of any sort. It was an outward activity—obedience reflected in action, not feelings. The centerpiece of her worship was prayer: fervent, anxious, and specific prayer. Her prayer was sad, agitated, and a little angry, but she talked to God anyway. In fact, she prayed so fervently that she appeared inebriated to Eli. God was the source of her problem, but she recognized that he was also the source of the solution, so she went along. While God at this point was her opponent in some important ways, her begrudging worship and prayer did acknowledge him as God. And God accepted her prayer on that basis.

This story clearly manifests our themes of covenant, sin, and redemption. First, God fulfilled his covenant by having given the people the land, which is productive through God's provision of fertility, and God is with them in the holy places where Elqanah and Hannah worship. Second, sin is easily found in the actions of Eli's sons and in Hannah's refusal of communion. Third, redemption is seen on many levels. Hannah is personally given reunion with God in worship and in the form of a baby. National redemption is found in the birth of the prophet who begins the process of anointing King Saul, who in turn begins the process of defeating the Philistines. Samuel also anoints King David, who completes the defeat of the Philistines and begins the dynasty which will culminate in the eternal rule of the Messiah, the Son of David. God's redemption in this story is many fold, both short range and long term.

Hannah immediately gains the companionship of God in worship, redeeming her from her self-imposed isolation from the divine. In the slightly longer term, she conceives and gives birth to Samuel and his brothers and sisters, redeeming her from childlessness. Some generations later, which Hannah, Peninah, and Elqanah probably didn't see, David becomes king of Israel and frees the Israelites from all invaders and foreign domination. Then further down the line, Jesus Christ, David's heir, brings eternal salvation. *All* of this began in Hannah's visit to the temple where she was severely disheartened but nevertheless looked for God and prayed.

God and Dagon

Israel was at war, under siege, and losing. The Philistines had defeated Israel's army and established garrisons throughout the land. The Philistines controlled the processing and sale of iron and charged extremely high prices for it, enriching themselves by impoverishing Israel. In Chapter 4 Israel tries a desperate attempt to break free and musters for a battle, taking the ark of the covenant with them.

The elders who decided to take the ark into battle were the authorities in Israel at that time and were responsible for nearly all aspects of life. They were the military commanders and had large authority in civil and religious affairs. The elders correctly deduced that the LORD had allowed them to be defeated, although the story does not say why or if some specific sin had been the cause of the lost battle. The elders' attribution of the defeat to God was correct, but their proposed solution was wrong. Their faulty thinking is seen clearly in their words in verse 3, "Let us bring the ark...that he [the LORD] may come among us and save us." Their desire for God's presence among them was legitimate, proper, and good, but their idea was to use the ark as a means of controlling God. They saw the ark as "God in a box," which could be carried around, thus ensuring God's presence. They wanted to control God. Instead of offering themselves as servants of God, they were trying to make God their servant.

Moses seems to have made a similar mistake at the burning bush when he asked to know God's name. The knowledge of God's true name was thought to confer some type of power over him, so Moses was seeking some level of control. As Adam named the animals, giving him dominion over them, Moses wanted to be able to be in charge of God by knowing his name, enabling him to call God to the scene. God wouldn't tell Moses his name and retained power. Moses and Israel were to be controlled *by* God, not in control *over* God. The Bible is very certain—things go well when God controls events. When humans try to take charge, not so much. The sin part of our trio of themes is quite evident in this part of the story.

The ark was housed in Shiloh and maintained by the Elide priests there. One of the threads of I Samuel is that the Levite priesthood of Shiloh had become corrupt and was using the priestly office for their own gain instead of leading Israel in obedience. Hophni and Phinehas continue contributing to that perception in this story. Instead of setting the elders straight about the presence of God and the ark, the priests agree to bring the ark to the camp and to use it as a means to try to ensure the presence of God and victory. This whole enterprise was perilously close to idolatry, treating a physical object as a god. While the ark was a holy object and a visible symbol of God's presence, God was totally distinct from the ark, and he was in no way defined by the ark. Israel was right to want God's presence among them, but they were willing to settle for a wooden box instead. It's not the same thing.

The result is a disaster. Israel's army is defeated badly, and the ark is captured by the Philistines and put in their temple as a war trophy. At this point Israel was very low. God's people were seemingly defeated and in retreat. The enemy had even taken the holiest object, the ark, which was Israel's sign of God being with them. Israel had been not only overthrown but humiliated and probably even felt abandoned by God, with good reason. If God is in control in the land of the Philistines, even in the temple of Dagon, as he proved, he is handling things on the battlefield where the ark is lost. So God intentionally took the ark out of Israel, taking away the most important sign and locus of his presence with his people. Small wonder that some Israelites simply gave up and joined with the Philistines (I Samuel 14:22).

The loss of the ark in this story is closely related both historically and theologically to the temple sermon passages in Jeremiah 7 and 26 in which Jeremiah prophesies about the coming destruction of the temple. He cites as evidence the destruction of the temple of Shiloh, which probably took place in the same military campaign as the loss of the ark. All of these passages warn against associating God with any physical object or relying on the holiness of a thing or place as conferring on humans any level of control over God.

In some ways, the church today can be seen as in a similar situation, if less drastically so. What was once called Christendom has been taken over by materialism, godlessness, and worldliness. The church is under siege in cultural terms and faces attacks from the secularists on a steady basis. Many people worship idols, especially the idols of money, status, entertainment, and possessions. Many of our oldest and most influential churches have become places where worship is not directed to God but to diversity, where sin and depravity are preached as good, and the only sin they recognize is judgmentalism. Sometimes the church feels like the faithful Israelites hiding in caves while society goes to hell around us. Too many Christians have adopted a "go-along, get-along" attitude and have effectively given up and joined with the forces opposing the church.

But, in I Samuel 4–6, while Israel feared that God had abandoned them, God was at work. He was out of sight and without fanfare at first but working to bring about his plan. And when

God takes on an idol, the idol loses. The ark was placed before the idol of Dagon as if it were an offering, but by morning the idol had fallen before the ark. They set the idol back up, and the next morning it had fallen again and was broken. To emphasize the point, God sent some kind of physical infirmity to the Philistines. And the Philistines were terrified and couldn't understand what was happening. When one leaves God out of their calculations, there will be an awful lot that can't be understood.

One clear principle applies to both Israel's situation and that of the current church. The kingdom of Satan is doing its utmost to destroy God's work, God's creation, and God's people. One of the key weapons in Satan's arsenal is despair. If he can get God's people to give up and quit trying, Satan has won an important battle. Despair destroys the effectiveness of God's people almost as effectively as physical destruction. The Israelites who went over to the Philistines had despaired of winning. So they abandoned Israel, and they abandoned God. Too many Christians are doing that today. It looks like materialism, illicit sex, and perversion are winning, so they become deeply depressed and stop trying to fight for God or to live for him. Even the Israelites who didn't abandon God gave up attempting to triumph and just hoped to survive by hiding and not being a target.

What they couldn't see was that God was very much at work and had already begun the process which would result in victory. The false god Dagon, which Israel was so afraid of, was at that very moment falling prostrate before the ark of the LORD of Hosts, God of Israel. And the Philistine idolaters were suffering physically for their contempt for God.

In addition, God had already called Samuel to be a prophet—a prophet who would issue God's call to two kings who would eventually overcome the Philistines and make Israel into the powerful nation which God intended it to be. God works on a lot of tracks at once.

Just as God triumphed over the idol, the kingdom of God will win over Satan. God and his heaven are not the least bit in danger from Satan. The devil can declare victory only over those humans who give in to him, but if we remain faithful to God and stay under his protection, Satan can't defeat us in the long run. We'll lose some skirmishes, and some of the losses will be very painful, but God has won the ultimate victory. We can be secure in our faith in that victory. This is the main meaning of the book of Revelation, which is summed up by Jesus in chapter 2, verse 10: "Be faithful unto death and I will give you the crown of life."

The Philistines made the same mistake as Israel in verse 7 and were frightened by the presence of the ark which they confused with God himself. They knew what God had done in Egypt during the Exodus and feared the same type of plagues on themselves. But they heeded their own advice. They took courage and acquitted themselves like soldiers and were victorious, capturing the ark as a spoil of war and apparently destroying the worship site at Shiloh, as is implied in Jeremiah 7.

The Philistines' mistake was furthered when they put their new war trophy in the temple of Dagon, their god. Apparently, they saw their military victory as a sign that their god Dagon had defeated Israel's God. So they placed the ark before the image of Dagon as an offering and as a statement of his superiority. In this they were badly mistaken, as they found when the next morning the image of Dagon was prostrated before the ark. So they set the idol back upright, thinking they had corrected the problem. God showed them the flaw in their thinking when the next morning the idol was again laid out before the ark with its head and hands broken off, emphasizing the powerlessness of the image. The people having to put Dagon back in his place shows a god who is dependent of humans when it should be the other way around. Isaiah 46:1–2 speaks to this: "Bel bows down, Nebo stoops, their idols are on beasts and cattle; these things you carry are loaded as burdens on weary beasts. They stoop, they bow down together, they cannot save the burden, but themselves go into captivity."

Dagon, being an inanimate object, was powerless against God and its loss of hands and head was a powerful symbol of that powerlessness. The physical infirmity which plagued the Philistines intensified the lesson. The biblical principle here is quite clear. Opposing God hurts.

In chapter 6 we see that even the idolaters know something about God. The priests of Dagon quickly recognize that the source of their problem was their attempt to mistreat the ark and their disrespect of Israel's God. They even recognize that recognition and restitution of their error were necessary parts of making things right. But their response was badly wrong. Instead of turning to God in repentance, they decided to send God far away. Jonah tried to run away from God while the Philistines tried to throw God away. Neither attempt was successful.

The Philistines and the modern secular materialists have some things in common. Both knew something about God. Both knew that their approaches to life were causing suffering. And both turned away from God to their false gods. The Philistines at least recognized the LORD as a god. Modern day godless idolaters deny the very existence of God. And they all continue to suffer or cause others to suffer. That part of the church which has nowadays decided to go along with secularism and materialism has become woefully ineffective.

What God's people must do to be effective is to return to God, obey him, be faithful to him, endure the hard times, reject despair, and continue to struggle for god's Kingdom. If we do that, we will see great things happen!

Looking ahead in the story of Israel in the Bible, Israel did that. Imperfectly, with a lot of false steps along the way, and far from unanimously, but they overall did it. Like Elkanah and Samuel, one person, one family holding true can make a huge difference for God's people as a whole. The nation of Israel committed some great sins and even finally had to be destroyed in order for God to get their attention, but there were always the faithful ones. Because of God's grace and work and through the faithfulness of the dedicated nation, Israel came out of the Babylonian captivity purged of idols and polytheism and ready to begin showing the world the one true God.

I am convinced that the church is about to go into captivity. Maybe not physical exile, but exile nonetheless. Like Israel, many will fall away because of the suffering; many will give in and simply become worldly. But God will preserve enough of his people and his church that those who are faithful through the trials, persecutions, and struggles will come out of the captivity and like Israel be ready for God's next great work.

The existence of a separate ark narrative which served as a source for the Deuteronomic history is a disputed issue in biblical studies.[32] If there is an ark narrative, the Deuteronomistic history expands upon it greatly and uses it in the service of the theology of Zion/David, temple/king as the centerpiece of God's salvation history. First Samuel 4 has Israel treating the ark nearly as a god, not simply a venerated object. The result—always the result of idolatry—is disaster. Second Samuel 5–6 offers counterpart stories to II Samuel 24, which is the obverse, in which the disasters of I Samuel 4 are reversed through David's obedience. Israel's sin brought the loss of the ark to the Philistines and the loss of what the Deuteronomic history saw as a national shrine at Shiloh. In II Samuel 6, David restores the ark and its symbolic presence of God to its proper place at the center of Israel. And in

---

32. L. Rost, *The Succession to the Throne of David* (ET M.D. Rutter and D.M. Gunn; Sheffield: Almond, 1982); A. F. Campbell, *The Ark Narrative:1 Sam. 4–6, 2 Sam. 6: A Form-Critical and Tradition-Historical Study* (SBLDS 16; Missoula: SBL and Scholars, 1975); P. D. Miller Jr. and J. J. M. Roberts, *The Hand of the* LORD: *A Reassessment of the 'Ark Narrative' of 1 Samuel* (Baltimore/ London: Johns Hopkins, 1977); A. Stirrup, "Why Has Yahweh Defeated Us Today Before The Philistines? The Question of The Ark Narrative," Tyndale Bulletin 51.1 (2000), 81–100.

II Samuel 5, David takes possession of Jerusalem, which will become the holy city. He also captures the Philistine idols, countering the events of I Samuel 4. In II Samuel 24, David inaugurates the ultimate national shrine which will become the Jerusalem temple, thereby bringing about the full culmination in the text of the complete Zion/David theme.

Redemption in this story takes two paths. One form of redemption is the return of the ark to Israel, confirming the presence of God with his people. The other track of redemption is the story's setting up of David's establishment of the worship site which would become the temple in Jerusalem, thus establishing the Zion/David combination which would be the centerpiece of God's ultimate redemptive activity in Jesus Christ.

David and Goliath

One of the most familiar stories in the Old Testament retold in song, poem, plays, comic books, movies, and even *Veggie Tales* is the story of David and Goliath. This story is a clear example of victory in the LORD's name. It contains much information about the historical and cultural situation of Israel which is useful in interpreting the text. There has been a drastic improvement in Israel's military situation since the events narrated in chapters 13 and 14. In that earlier period Saul was able to muster only six hundred soldiers to fight (13:15). This necessitated his fighting an irregular guerrilla warfare consisting of raids and assassinations. The Israelites hid "in caves and in holes and in rocks and in tombs and in cisterns." This could well have been for tactical reasons rather than simply fear. Typical guerrilla hit-and-run tactics mandate such hiding before and after a raid.

In I Samuel 17, Israel now can field an organized army in large formation and engage in open battle against the Philistine invaders. There is a definite military structure to Israel's force, with officers and schedules. Also, there is a reasonably sophisticated logistical operation in place. David makes repeated trips to the army, bringing supplies from home, including supplies for the officers over the Bethlehem contingent. The supplies were delivered to a logistics officer, the "keeper of the baggage," strongly indicating a centralized distribution system. That this system was working effectively is attested by the forty days in which Goliath came out to challenge Israel. While the forty days are probably not to be taken as a literal mathematical quantity, it indicates a lengthy period, requiring a steady supply of a large amount of food and water for the soldiers.

Saul was much more successful than the usual cursory reading or comic book Bible ideas would indicate. First Samuel 14:47–48 clearly states that Saul won his wars against Israel's enemies, specifically including the Philistines. The best evidence that Saul prevailed against the Philistines is that after his death, Israel engaged in a civil war, and the Philistines made no real attempt to exploit the situation.

Frequently, Saul's success is unseen because of his role in the story as a foil to David. Saul's reign was transitional, an important step in Israel's moving from a tribal society to a strong central monarchical government under David. This period is an important element of the story of David's rise to kingship and greatness. In the view of the Bible, Saul is a placeholder, serving as a part of the means by which David rose to power. Saul played a major role in David's preparation when he recognized David's abilities and gave him opportunities to excel in military service. Saul promoted David as a result of David's successes.[33] All of these historical and military facets are important to God's covenant with Israel.

---

33. Even David's promotion is made to appear to Saul's discredit by the staunchly pro-David writers. David is moved from a headquarters job to command of a combat unit. While David's new position is more dangerous, it is also a much higher-profile job with great opportunity. Most likely, David had been angling to get that job ever since the giant fell down. To see it in modern terms, an ambitious general in the Pentagon during wartime would gladly leave the safety of headquarters to get command of a division in combat. David was definitely ambitious, and Saul gave David the opportunity to achieve much of this young man's goals.

Israel's improved military and political situations are presented in the Bible generally as the result of God keeping his covenant with Israel. The Deuteronomic history in particular sees military victory as God's covenant faithfulness and military defeat as God's punishment for Israel's covenant violations. Judges 2 and II Kings 17 are particularly straightforward statements to this effect. Instances of God's covenant faithfulness abound in this story. Israel's army gathering in well-organized formation indicates less Philistine domination than in chapters 13–14. Like the exodus from Egypt, God looks on the oppression of his covenant people and is acting to end it.

King Saul and Israel's success against the Philistines (14:47–48) has effected considerable independence from the Philistines. God and Israel's military are in the process of freeing Israel from Philistine domination, and King Saul was a significant part of this process. First Samuel 14:47–48 is a clear statement of Saul's overall military and political accomplishments and victories. Those, which were due to Israel's much better military and greater political and economic freedom, are presented as the result of God's actions under the covenant. Israel's battles are apparently seen as holy wars in which God is the primary agent, and victory in battle is gained through God's participation for Israel's sake. Deuteronomy 20:4 sees Israel's battles in this light, and the conquest stories also show God doing battle for Israel (Deuteronomy 2–3; Joshua 1:2–3; Judges 1:2–24). David's statement that Israel's military is composed of the "armies of the living God" reflects this idea that Israel's wars are holy wars fought on God's behalf and with God as a combatant.

Covenant is the basic idea behind the presentation of David's speeches to the soldiers and to Saul. His statement that the LORD saved him from the bear and the lion is an allusion to the promise God made to David through Samuel that David would be king. It is also a foreshadowing of the Zion/David covenant which God announced through the prophet Nathan in II Samuel 7. God is protecting David from predators and from Goliath and the Philistines. God's ultimate redemption is to come through David and his descendants, which requires David to survive to become king. The national covenant which David also implies is upheld by God through David's defeat of the giant and also through the victory of the Israelite army over the Philistines. Israel's well-equipped army strongly implies good agricultural production, which was God's fulfilling his covenant promise to Israel of a land flowing with milk and honey.

Sin is found in the story when the soldiers of Israel were afraid to face the giant to the extent of being unwilling to do so. The fear itself wasn't a sin. Being afraid to do battle with a giant soldier who is well trained is not cowardice but wisdom. Such fear is unavoidable. It is highly probable that David was quite afraid when he went out to face Goliath. But he went out anyway. Feeling afraid isn't sin; giving in to fear can be a sin, however. David conquered his fears as well as conquering the Philistine. Fear and doubt are not the opposite of faith but an integral part of faith. David overcame his fear enough to volunteer to fight Goliath and to think clearly enough to devise a tactical plan which was highly practical and did not require a miracle. "'Not by might nor by power, but by My Spirit,' says the LORD of hosts" (Zechariah 4:6). David's words reflect this concept, but he still took a judicious approach as well. David's plan was simple: stay out of the reach of Goliath's weapons. Using the sling's range, David was able to attack the giant from far enough away that Goliath's huge weapons could not be brought into play.

Redemption is found in this story in several ways and on several levels. The surface level is seen in David's victory and his personal survival. At the national level, Israel won a major battle and turned back an invading army, increasing Israel's level of independence from the Philistines. The Deuteronomic history consistently equates military victory with redemption. On a longer-range, spiritual level, this story shows David's first steps on the path to the monarchy. That journey takes a very circuitous route with some serious missteps but ultimately moves to the Davidic kingship and dynasty, the establishment of Mount Zion as the holiest of holy places, and ultimately to eternal salvation through Jesus Christ.

Faith in God is an important element of redemption, as we've seen over and over again. David had large amounts of belief and trust, but part of his faith was based on his confidence in his own skill with his sling. He didn't test God by relying on a miracle. He didn't do something stupid and call it "stepping out in faith." He made the best plan he could devise and made it work. His plan depended on his own training and the many hours of practice with his weapon. Even miracles are improved by hard work. The plan worked quite well. David won the duel. The rock sank into Goliath's forehead, apparently penetrating his skull. While that could well have been a fatal wound, David's beheading of the giant removed all doubt.

While there is some tension among the texts regarding David's rise to prominence as one of the servants of Saul, they are all in agreement that David was a highly competent soldier who rose through Israel's army and that he was being groomed by God for historical impact.

David and the Ark

In the previous section on I Samuel 4–6, we saw the troubles that resulted from treating the ark in near idolatrous fashion and trying to control God. Second Samuel 6 is the continuation of the hypothetical ark narrative, and in this section, King David gets it right. Mostly.

Since the events in I Samuel 6, the ark had resided in obscurity in the village of Kiriath-jearim and had played little, if any, role in Israelite national affairs. (At least it played no role that made it into our present text.) However, David's desire to bring the ark to Jerusalem was based on an impulse that was proper and correct. He wanted God in his capital city, and since the ark was the visible symbol of God's presence, moving the object to a worship center in Jerusalem was appropriate.

While David and the elders in I Samuel 4 both tried to insure God's presence by having the ark with them, there is a significant difference. The Israelites in I Samuel 4 were trying to be in control and wanted to force God to bless their military efforts. In contrast, David's intention was to honor the LORD and bring God's holy artifact back from obscurity to a prominent place in the religious affairs of David's government and the nation as a whole. It could be said that David, instead of trying to control God, was putting himself under God's control, and that the ark was brought to Jerusalem in order that God might supervise King David.

One thing is clear: David wanted something good. He desired everybody to share in God's presence through the ark, which would be housed at the national capital city in a royal worship site. This is a clear example of the covenant. God promised his blessings, and his ark was a tangible sign of him being there. David wanted the ark in Jerusalem as a sign of his obedience to the covenant and to God. That David had political motives and goals as well doesn't eliminate his devout purposes. As king, David had to consider the political implications of everything he did.

In both cases, I Samuel 4-6 and II Samuel 6, the physical ark was closely connected with the desire for God to be with his people. While that idea might sound uncomfortably like magic or even idolatry to the modern mind, we are too quick in judgment. God often makes himself known to humanity through physical objects. Beautiful art has long been a useful worship aid (even ugly art—see Matthias Gruenewald's Isenheim altarpiece). Albrecht Durer's praying hands and the wonderful paintings of Warner Sallman have been precious to many believers for use in worship and devotion. The altar of a church is often thought to be a physical place of increased holiness. The greatest instance of God blessing physical things as carriers of holiness is the incarnation of Jesus Christ in which "the Word was made flesh and dwelt among us."

So physical objects being seen as bearers of holiness and as holy themselves is a perfectly acceptable biblical idea and is not at all directly connected with idolatry. While neither God nor his coming among his people was in any way limited to the ark, the ark was holy and was a reminder of God's presence. The modern idea that the ark was symbolic of God's presence is a reasonable way to understand the attitude of Israel to the ark, even though as we saw in I Samuel 4, the Israelite elders did not see it as simply symbolic. The ark, then, was but a wooden box, although ordained by God to be the sign and hub of his walk with his children of Israel. It was holy and as such was to be touched and carried only by the Levite priests, who were sanctified as a holy tribe by their actions at Mount Sinai in the golden calf incident. The holy Levites could handle the holy ark, and both Levite and ark mediated God to the Israelite people.

The concept of the ark which was held by Israel varies from text to text. One point of view sees the ark as a war palladium with God inside it. This is the idea found in some of the stories in the book of Joshua. In these, Levites carried the ark in front of the rest of the Israelite people moving across the Jordan, and it was also the sanctified object borne front and center in the processions around Jericho. The shrine at Shiloh seems to derive its holiness from the "ark of the LORD of hosts who sits enthroned on the cherubs." Samuel sleeps by the ark in the attempt to determine if God would speak to him. The elders in I Samuel 4 clearly see the ark as a war token, even though the point of the story is that they were mistaken. All of these stories envision a very close connection between the physical ark and God's presence, possibly to the point that God and the ark are indistinguishable. This concept can also be found in Psalm 24, which is widely thought to have been used for the entry of the ark into the sacred precincts of the temple. "The King of glory shall come in" is the reply when it is the ark that was entering during a procession.

In a sense, the ark is the locus of the covenant between God and Israel. "I will be your God" (Jeremiah 30:22 [c.f. Exodus 6:7]) is the central guarantee of the covenant, and the ark is the physical embodiment of the fulfillment of that promise. God and David are both being faithful to God's covenant with Israel. The theme of covenant is certainly present in this story. In contrast, Deuteronomy sees the ark as less the direct presence of God and more as a simple chest, functioning simply as a receptacle for the tablets and book of the law (Deuteronomy 10:31). It does not seem to be closely identified with God's spirit being with Israel, and holiness is more closely tied to the law than to the ark.

At the other extreme, the priestly writings portray the ark as a grand, ornate, gold-plated centerpiece of the tabernacle. There, it is the idealized ark of the testimony, with the covenant being separate from the physical object. In exilic and post-exilic Israel, the covenant exists, and God is showing himself to Israel completely aside from the ark. This probably indicates that the ark was no longer in existence when the texts were finalized, necessitating the theological idea that God's presence with Israel in the covenant and the ark were separable.

The holiness of the ark is part of a series of structures in Israelite theology encompassing ark, temple, priesthood, Jerusalem, and the big rock which was the scene of David's encounter with God in II Samuel 24 and which probably became the floor of the Holy of Holies in the Jerusalem temple. Much of this orderly concept of holiness is announced in the Deuteronomistic history in a convoluted string of stories which seem to have arisen against the background of priestly politics, civic quests for superiority, competing temples, stewards of holy sites trying to best each other, and Josianic era political maneuvering. The intertwined threads of the traditions, texts, and narratives cannot be untangled with any certainty, even though some of the rival lines can be seen: Shiloh/Jerusalem, Levite/Zadokite, tribal ark/royal temple, and tribal elders/king can all be discerned in the ark narratives and in the Deuteronomistic history as a whole. Great effort and ingenuity have been employed in the attempt to discover the timeline of all these events and to explicate the text responsibly.[34] While

------

34. L. Rost, *The Succession to the Throne of David* (ET M.D. Rutter and D.M. Gunn; Sheffield: Almond, 1982), 1-9; A. F. Campbell, *The Ark Narrative, 1 Sam 4–6, 2 Sam 6: A Form-Critical and Tradition-Historical Study* (SBLDS 16; Missoula: SBL and Scholars, 1975), 1–54; P. D. Miller, Jr. and J. J. M. Roberts, *The Hand of the* LORD: *A Reassessment of the 'Ark Narrative' of 1 Samuel* (Baltimore/London: Johns Hopkins, 1977), 2–6.

several of these attempts have produced interesting results, the lack of any general agreement other than the existence of a vaguely defined ark narrative gives little credibility to the proposed details. Once again, we are left with the current, finished text as the primary certainty with the notional earlier forms and versions of the stories too fragmentary and theoretical to be very useful in interpreting the biblical story.

Our text in verses 6:1–2 (also in I Samuel 4:4) makes clear the strong connection between the ark and the title "LORD of Hosts" and adds in the formula "who sits enthroned on the cherubim." The term *hosts* of which God is the lord has multiple meanings. The basic one is military in nature and refers to an army of some sort in which God is the lord and marks the presence of the host of heaven and also is the lord of the armies of Israel.[35] There is probably a connection between the military connotations of the title "LORD of Hosts" and the statement in 6:1 that the congregation which gathered to move the ark was a military formation. Yahweh is the lord of the hosts of Israel, and it was representatives of that military host who accompanied the ark of the LORD of Hosts on its journey to Jerusalem.

Israel often thought of their God as a warrior deity, and therefore Israel's wars were holy wars in which God fought on the side of Israel. The book of Joshua shows this most clearly. Joshua 1:2 and 6 state that Israel's conquest of the land was the result of God giving it to them, not through their military prowess alone. The fall of the walls of Jericho also shows this concept of the gift of the land through God's fighting on Israel's behalf. Israel's actions at Jericho consisted of marching around the city, led by the Levites and the ark, blowing of trumpets, and ritual shouts. These actions hardly constitute sound military tactics and look much more like worship ceremonies. The city walls crumble through the direct act of God, not through men's conduct, and

---

35. B. W. Anderson, "Hosts," *Interpreters' Dictionary of the Bible* (Nashville: Abingdon, 1962), 654–656.

Israel makes its first gain west of the Jordan through the activities of their warrior God. The ark certainly functions as a war protection in the Jericho story, similar to the way that the elders in I Samuel 4 tried to use it, but again, the difference is in who is seen as being in control. God commanded the use of the ark in the battle at Jericho, but in I Samuel 4, Israel was trying to command God.[36]

The holiness of the ark did not derive solely from its martial aspects, but from the presence of God in the physical ark. God was thought to be invisibly inside the wooden box, which was covered by the cherubs which were on its lid (I Samuel 4:4; Psalm 80:1; 99:1; Isaiah 37:16) The LORD was also thought to be enthroned on the cherubs or riding on them (II Samuel 22:11; Psalm 18:2). A closely related modern idea is found in the hymn line "his chariots of wrath the deep thunderclouds form." So although the ark was a throne of God; it did not contain God inside the wood of its construction.

David and the chosen men of Israel were making merry, as seen in verse 5. They were hootin' and hollerin' with all their might, having a lot of fun, accompanied by loud music and dancing. But the celebration was not just noise and fun. It was a worship service, not just letting loose (it was a letting loose, too). But the center was the ark and the presence of God.

The celebration came to a sudden end in verse 8 when Uzzah died after touching the ark. It is not stated why this caused his death. The usual idea is that his demise was because he was not a Levite. If so, why did the Philistines who carried the ark around not die? We simply are not told, and any answer is speculative. We are told only of an event and the people's reaction to it. So we can't be certain that Uzzah's death was due to some sin on his part, although God's anger hints strongly in that direction.

---

36. C. L. Seow, "Ark of the Covenant," *Anchor Bible Dictionary*, ed. D. N. Freedman (New York: Doubleday, 1992), I 388.

We are told clearly that Uzzah's expiration put a damper on the celebration and ended the procession to Jerusalem.

The focus here is on David and his response—he was afraid of God and angry, justifiably and rightly so. David's emotions were not sin, though. It appears that David sinned here, but not by being perturbed and frightened. Those were understandable, and God was okay about it. Job was also angry and afraid of God and said so very openly and at length (Job 6:4–13; 9:11–24; etc.). God's response to Job's fury and accusations was to tell Job's friends, "You have not spoken of me what is right, as my servant Job has" (Job 42:7).

David's sin was not anger. It was not a sin to be afraid. David let his feelings lead him into the sin of ceasing to seek God. David thought, "God is a dangerous God, and I'd better not get too close to him." That was wrong, however. What should have been David's proper response is "God is a dangerous God, so I'd better be nice to him and stay on his good side." That's not wrong either, but it's not enough. It is indeed good to avoid provoking God into bringing disaster, but God wanted David's willing love, not just a placating attempt.

David's response to Uzzah's death was disquietingly similar to that of the Philistines when they realized that the ark was dangerous. Both of them separated themselves from the ark and at least symbolically from the presence of God. David chose to leave the ark with a local household and abandon his plans to bring the venerated object into his own city.

Once again, the ark was not in its proper place with God's people, as had previously happened when it was captured by the Philistines. This time there was a great difference. Instead of bringing suffering, the ark caused Obed-Edom to be blessed. What form the benevolence took is not stated, but its relation to "all that belongs to him" implies that it included earthly prosperity.

So David goes and gets the ark back—not David's finest moment. David seems to be greedy and jealous. He lets Obed-Edom take the risk of having the dangerous ark in his house, but when it proved to be a boon, David retrieves it so he himself can get the blessing. The theme of sin is seen in this part of the story. Not only his envy was sinful, but so was David's giving up on bringing the ark with the presence of God to his capital. His rather callous possible endangerment of Obed-edom was also not in keeping with the commandment to love thy neighbor as thyself.

Ironically, David does better than this later when embroiled further in sin. After conceiving a child with the wife of Uriah, the son dies, and David's response is to worship (II Samuel 12). So David somewhere in the stories learned a very important lesson. God is a great, holy, loving, and dangerous God who is worthy of our worship. David seems to have profited from his mistakes, improved, and matured spiritually. That is a key to David's success—obedience and seeking God's presence. Like all humans, David often had to practice these in repentance, but God accepts David's true remorse and restores to David the joy of God's salvation.

Another of the success stories of modern biblical scholarship is the insight that Joshua, Judges, I and II Samuel, and I and II Kings are a literary unit which reveals the legal perspective of the book of Deuteronomy. This Deuteronomistic history was clearly identified by Martin Noth.[37] Recently, two editions of the Deuteronomistic history have been identified by Cross and Nelson. The earlier edition was the primary one and was intended to be programmatic for the reform of King Josiah found in II Kings 22–23.[38] The second edition was minimally intrusive and related the fall of Jerusalem with not much theologizing.[39]

---

37. Martin Noth, *The Deuteronomistic History*, Sheffield, JSOT Supplement Series, 1981, 4–11.

38. F. M. Cross, *Canaanite Myth and Hebrew Epic* (Cambridge: Harvard University Press, 1973), 287; Richard D. Nelson, *The Double Redaction of the Deuteronomistic History*, Sheffield, JSOT Supplement Series, 1981, 121–122.

39. Cross, *Canaanite Myth*, 288; Nelson, *The Double Redaction*, 122–123.

The use of the ark narrative by the Deuteronomistic historians fits the theory of its having been constructed of older materials to serve as support for the reform of Josiah. A main element of Deuteronomy, the Deuteronomistic history, and Josiah's reform was the centralization of all Israelite sacrifice in the temple at Jerusalem. The ark was the carrier of God's presence for the old tribal league, and Zion/Jerusalem was the center of God's presence for the Davidic monarchy. David brought the ark to Jerusalem and by doing so merged the two major seats of the presence of God. For the Deuteronomists, this was a perfect method of showing that Jerusalem was the sole focus of God and that Jerusalem's temple was therefore the ultimate and only true holy place. Another major piece in this series of stories involving the ark is the tale of the plague in II Samuel 24. This narrative serves in the Deuteronomistic history as God's confirmation of Zion as the supreme sanctified place. With this account, all the pieces are now in place in Jerusalem for the Deuteronomists: ark, tabernacle, and threshing floor where God met with David. The stage is prepared for the construction of Solomon's temple which will establish an eternal presence of God with his people and David's eternal dynasty with Zion as the centerpiece.

The recognition that God had selected Zion as the site of his temple is the element of redemption in this story and a major part of the redemption in the Deuteronomistic History and the whole Old Testament. Important sections of the New Testament also share in the idea of the holiness of Zion. The announcement of the birth of John the Baptist took place inside the temple. Several noteworthy events in the book of Acts take place in the temple compound. Jesus taught in the temple and parts of his trial were probably held there on the grounds in the sacred precincts. In the utmost story of redemption, Jesus died near Jerusalem, the hallowed city, very near where David first placed the ark.

Jeroboam

The story of Jeroboam is an excellent example of the principle of letting the text speak for itself instead of imposing meaning on the material. Too often we interpret our perceptions of the text, or worse, interpret the interpretations we have heard from others. Most of us come to this story about Jeroboam with the idea already in our minds that Jeroboam is the villain. After all, he's the one who initiated the golden calves and the "sin which he caused Israel to sin"; therefore; he's the worst kind of idolater.

While that view isn't totally untrue, it isn't the whole story by any means. As we shall see, there is much more to the story. Jeroboam is a complex character with many desirable qualities and performs several admirable acts, but all of that will be missed if we see him simply as the one-dimensional bad guy instead of the multiple-layered, round character which he actually is.

We first meet Jeroboam in I Kings 11 where he is an impressive young member of the Solomonic regime but with an interesting twist: he is an Ephraimite and the son of a widow. In a dynasty in which Judeans and especially Jerusalemites are heavily overrepresented, for a member of the tribe of Ephraim to rise to a position of great prominence, power, and prestige is quite a testimony to Jeroboam's talents, desire to succeed, and political skills (and self-promotional abilities, as well). To have accomplished this as the son of a widow and therefore without a father to serve as a patron in the government is doubly impressive.

Jeroboam was clearly a very talented administrator and was recognized as such. As a result, he was given tasks and employment commensurate with his potential. He was on the fast track and moving up. God had given him a tremendous gift of administration (I Cor. 12:28), and Jeroboam wasn't about to hide his candle under a bushel. He had been given great innate capability and competence, and he had acquired ambition to match.

But when he is introduced, he is putting those God-given attributes to a highly questionable use: he is supervising the work of those Israelites who had been subjected to forced labor on Solomon's building projects. Solomon's form of compulsory service was probably a larger system similar in concept to the limited one described in I Kings 5:13–14. In that regime, Israelites worked one month out of three in Lebanon preparing materials for Solomon's royal buildings. This labor was seen by the royal establishment as a form of taxation and was therefore performed without pay.[40] In fact, this was probably a similar system to the one which had been imposed on Israel by Egypt in Exodus 1.[41] This servitude in Egypt had been viewed by both God and Israel as slavery, and God sent the plagues to Egypt in order to end this unjust oppression to which God's covenant people had been subjected. While Solomon's purposes were basically good (and even Pharaoh's purposes weren't evil), the means he chose to

---

40. Israel and the ancient Near East had no standard of currency, so taxes were mostly collected in goods. The forced labor was simply a way of collecting taxes in the form of labor instead of goods. While such a system makes good economic sense, Israelite tribal society saw it as slavery and oppression.

41. M. Noth, *Exodus* (Philadelphia: Westminster, 1962), 20; W. Dever, *Did God Have a Wife?*, 282; R. Albertz, *A History of Israelite Religion in the Old Testament Period* (Louisville: Westminster/John Knox, 1994), 141-143; J. Alberto Soggin, "Compulsory Labor Under David and Solomon," *Studies in the Period of David and Solomon*, ed. Tomoo Ishida, (Winona Lake: Eisenbrauns, 1982).

accomplish them were not acceptable in the eyes of the tribes of Israel.

In this instance, both Solomon and Jeroboam were misusing their authority and their abilities and were abusing Israel against God's wishes. But just like in Egypt in the book of Exodus, God was neither ignorant of the situation nor absent from it. God was very aware of the conditions and was at work on a plan to end the subjugation and mistreatment of his people. He began his liberation of Israel by again issuing a call, this time to Jeroboam.

God had given Jeroboam great leadership skills, and since these were intended for securing freedom, God went to extraordinary lengths to persuade Jeroboam to change from oppressor to instrument of God's release of his people. God intended for Jeroboam to end the misuse of his aptitude and industriousness for Jeroboam's own personal advancement and to put them to work in a special mission, the unshackling of all God's people. God can be accurately described as the deity who gives second chances—and third, fourth. . . [see the stories of David, Abraham, Peter, etc.]), and God is giving Jeroboam another try to serve a divine purpose instead of his own aspirations.

The first step in this plan of which we are told was when Ahijah the prophet was sent to Jeroboam with a message from God. This message and commission turned Jeroboam's life around thoroughly. It had a ripple effect not only for his daily actions but also for his status and his role in Israel's history. It would eventually bring about a major transformation in Israel, as well. Although God's calls don't normally tell people to launch a rebellion and become king, they do tend to result in radical metamorphoses of the people he calls, like Moses, Gideon, David, Peter, Augustine, Martin Luther, and a host of others.

Ahijah delivered not only a message to Jeroboam—he did so through a sign, a symbolic (or ecstatic) act which pointed to God's call and made the message one that Jeroboam could not ignore. This sign entails Ahijah's destruction of a new cloak, dividing it into twelve pieces and inviting Jeroboam to take ten of the pieces standing for God's intention of giving ten tribes to Jeroboam as a kingdom. This tearing apart of a new garment gives Ahijah a significant economic investment in the message since cloaks were rather expensive in materials and time to weave and tailor (see Judges 17 where the well-paid Levite priest gets one new suit of clothes each year). This event doesn't fill the entire message but emphasizes the actual message to Jeroboam from God which comes in four parts.

The first part is that God has chosen Jeroboam to be king over a major portion of his chosen people, Israel This was not about his self-aggrandizement and pleasure. It's about achievement of tasks to advance God's work. This is a pattern in the Bible (and in life) in which God gives talents and abilities to a person in order to enable the person to carry out the divine plan. When the person uses those gifts as God intends, blessings result. When the talents are used simply for personal gain, troubles result. David and Solomon are both examples of this. Like Jeremiah who had been prepared from conception for his prophetic vocation (Jeremiah 1:5), Jeroboam had been equipped for a great work and then is notified that the work for which he has been selected and readied by God is to be king over the large majority of God's people.

This is a pattern we see often in the Bible. Moses, Gideon, Joshua, David, and Jehu among others all show a similar God-given skill set and commission. Each of these men and Jeroboam rose to accomplish great things, and each failed in some important areas. But in every case, God worked with these imperfect humans, with these jars of clay. In the fallen world we live in, God works with what he's got, and that's Jeroboam, Moses, and David. And we see that God accomplished very much when these flawed imperfect human beings answered the call and obeyed, even if not ideally.

The second part of God's message delivered by Ahijah concerns God's condemnation of Solomon's polytheism and God's rejection of Solomon because of that apostasy. This censure of Solomon because of his tolerance of polytheism is a strikingly strong one. God says that in condoning the worship of other gods, Solomon has "forsaken" the LORD by allowing the worship of false gods. Solomon had fallen into that which proved such a temptation to Israel for so long. That was the sin of taking up the Canaanite view of Yahweh as the high God and as the divine king of a host of lesser gods. In this view, worshiping other gods wasn't a rejection of the LORD but was simply a recognition that there were lesser divinities who were under Yahweh's authority but with their own spheres of influence and who had to be dealt with in those areas. In this view, the worship of Baal, the fertility god, was appropriate since Yahweh had delegated those fecundity functions to his son Baal; therefore, worshiping Baal was a part of the worship of Yahweh. Other gods could be addressed in a similar theological construction. Ahijah, the prophets, the Levites, and God himself all responded to this approach with a resounding "NO!" God's instructions to Israel through the law, the prophets, and the true priests were crystal clear that Israel was to worship no other gods of any sort, at any time, or under any theological covers. God's people must maintain exclusive fidelity to God with no exceptions or reservations. They either knew Yahweh as the one and only true God, or they rejected him, forsaking him for polytheism. God is not the high god but the *only* God and absolute;. Exclusive loyalty to the one God is a non-negotiable requirement for his people.

Solomon had failed to maintain that fidelity and, as a result, his descendants would lose the rule of the majority of Israelites. Clearly God takes covenant fidelity very seriously; he sees sin, and he judges it. It is also patent that sin has consequences which are not limited to the person who commits the sin but affect other people as well. Unfortunately, Solomon's sin affected not only himself but his whole family, his descendants for many generations, and virtually all of the citizens of the kingdom of Israel.

In contrast, Jeroboam is obviously being called to the exclusive worship of the LORD God, and he is told to avoid the sins of polytheism and idolatrous worship activities, which Solomon had practiced. In his royal career, Jeroboam would do a good job of avoiding polytheism but not so well at maintaining proper worship practices when he reinforced practices such as high places and images such as golden calves which were prohibited in Deuteronomy.

A very cogent underlying assumption in this section is the standard Israelite theological concept that God is at work in Israel and is directing its national life toward his good purpose. This not only affects matters that are overtly religious but also equally involves functions and matters that we would think of as purely political. God is adamant that he wants to direct not only the religious life of his people and his chosen nation but its entire life in all its aspects. The covenant code in Exodus 20:21–23:33 and the book of Deuteronomy contain a lot of what we would consider secular law, indicating that Israel and God did not make a distinction between sacred law and secular law. This all-inclusive demand of fidelity and conformity by his people to God is also seen in his judgment on Solomon. The king's infidelity in spiritual matters had great and far-reaching results in political terms.

The third element of Ahijah's message to Jeroboam is that God is going to keep his word through the covenant, even when humans do not. Judah would remain as the Davidic kingdom because God abided by his everlasting oath to David (II Samuel 7, Psalm 89, 132), but Solomon's sins of falling away from the faith brought the repercussions which caused a severe loss to the Davidic dynasty and Judah.

In the fourth element of God's message, Jeroboam is told by God to be firmly obedient to the holy ordinances in the same manner that David had done and which Solomon had not.

Jeroboam receives a pledge as well as a command, but the vow is conditional. "If you will hearken to all that I command you, and will walk in my ways, and do what is right in my eyes by keeping my statute and my commandments, as David my servant did, I will be with you, and will build for you a sure house." God's elevation of Jeroboam was tied to a particular responsibility, and his assurance to Jeroboam is tied to Jeroboam's performance of that duty. Jeroboam is to be the king of Israel not in just a political sense but in a religious sense too. He is to lead Israel in the proper acknowledgement of the true God as well.

God's word to Jeroboam entails power, authority, and dynasty, but it includes an even greater promise: "I will be with you." God's presence with Jeroboam and Israel is the greatest pledge given by the Father in the message, but it too is conditional upon Jeroboam and Israel keeping the laws which God set out as specific covenant guidelines. This is the standard by which all the kings were to be judged, and Israel as a people will be evaluated with by the same benchmark. If Jeroboam and Israel will be obedient, they will receive God's blessings, including the experience of God's being with them.

To this point, Jeroboam has been the relatively uninvolved recipient of God's message, but in keeping with what we have seen of his character, his inactivity ends, and he begins to show the qualities which make him initially an admirable follower of God. Jeroboam possessed several good traits that had been given to him and he put those attributes to proper use. He had been equipped with what was necessary, and when Jeroboam began to use those qualities for God, good things resulted.

Jeroboam's character tended to make him a *participant* instead of a mere observer; he tended to do something instead of watching. When he received God's message through Ahijah, Jeroboam shows by his deeds before and after the message that passivity was not his style. Jeroboam not only received the message, he went to work; he not only heard God's plan, he participated in it and tried to make it come about. For Jeroboam, his tendency toward action was a natural talent, but he still had to put that ability to work and be willing to take a big risk in listening to God. For some others, this participation was harder than for Jeroboam. Jeremiah, Jonah, and Moses tried to avoid God's call, and Isaac withdrew from conflict, but such lack of involvement was not in Jeroboam's character. Jeroboam accepted the call of God and immediately went into action.

This attempt to actively obey God resulted in Jeroboam beginning some sort of rebellion of which we are only told that he "lifted up his hand against the king." For unexpressed reasons, the rebellion was unsuccessful, and Jeroboam was forced to flee for his life. Jeroboam complied with God but failed to become king or even to maintain his place in Israel. This seems to contradict the grandiose promises of Ahijah's speech, but only if it is viewed from too short a perspective. God wanted Jeroboam to achieve success, and that happened, but it came on God's schedule, not on Jeroboam's. What appeared to be a blunder was only a delay—a temporary setback, not complete failure.

In spite of this letdown, Jeroboam's character was strong and deep enough that he did not let an initial failure bring an end to his determination to obey God and gain power. He was *practical* enough to recognize his lack of success, and his response was equally pragmatic. In order to escape the death sentence passed on him by Solomon, Jeroboam fled from Israel and went to Egypt, preserving his life and at least the potential of achieving his goal at a later date. His wise nature told him that it was not the right time and that his attempt to become king had flopped. His useful response was not in leaning on the everlasting arms, nor turning it all over to God, nor doing something silly and calling it "stepping out on faith." Instead he ran: hard, fast, and far. His best defense was to put a lot of distance between himself and his adversary. This was not a heroic response, nor the stuff of a pious martyr legend, but it was eminently functional. Jeroboam had enough sense to know when something was not working. This did not reveal a lack of faith in God's promise but was based on a high degree of trust. By fleeing, Jeroboam kept God's option open. He knew that martyrs don't become kings afterward, and his eye (and God's) was on the throne. Jeroboam's faith that God would give him the office required his survival, and Jeroboam took the smart method of ensuring his life: crossing the international boundary out of Solomon's jurisdiction. In this case a sensible response was a faithful response.

Once in Egypt, Jeroboam proved himself possessed of another virtue by being *patient*. Waiting surely did not come easy to a person as action oriented as Jeroboam, but it was required of him in this stage of God's plan. He ran away to Egypt, but there in exile he waited and watched for another opportunity. Another chance would come, and Jeroboam would make the most of it, but it would show up on God's schedule, and Jeroboam would have to sit tight, honing his patience.

Jeroboam was willing to wait but not simply passively accepting of whatever came. As we saw earlier, idleness was not in Jeroboam's nature. But his forbearance coupled with his *persistence* stood him in good stead. We see Jeroboam's willingness to defer his ambition and that he was apparently even willing to acquiesce in the tribes' acceptance of Rehoboam as king (as we see in his being amenable to Rehoboam's desire for three days to consider his response to the tribes' request). But Jeroboam's patience was not indecision or uncertainty. He maintained a constancy of purpose, and while he was willing to wait for his goal to be achieved, he remained resolute in working toward it. He suffered setbacks and delays, but they did not shake him from his purpose to which God had called him.

Solomon's death made possible the next stage in Jeroboam's path to the kingship. Solomon's heir as king of Judah and Jerusalem and presumptive heir as king over Israel was Rehoboam, who went to Shechem to meet with the tribes and all Israel with the intention of being confirmed as king over all of them. Jeroboam took a great risk in attending this meeting, but he went. He had been commissioned to be the nation's ruler, and he worked toward that goal and took logical steps to achieve it, even at grave peril to himself. When Jeroboam was obedient and in accord with God's wishes, God provided means and opportunity for Jeroboam to accomplish the divinely given task. First Kings 12:15 definitely shows that God was in the assembly at Shechem and that he was very much at work in Israel's national and daily lives trying to bring about his will. Jeroboam was a key element in that will. In response, Jeroboam put himself in a precarious spot, but he was *present* where God wanted him. Somebody once said that 90 percent of life is just showing up. While that certainly is an overly optimistic view, making one's appearance is at least a minimum requirement. For Jeroboam, simply being at Shechem was dangerous since he was under sentence of death. But he came anyway and so was available where and when God wanted him.

Jeroboam was not simply there, he was a participant in the proceedings, even to the point of being in the forefront of the Israelite tribes' delegation. Prudence and a concern for his personal safety might have dictated a lower profile there, even anonymity, but his task and his plan necessitated his assuming a leadership role, and he did so.

Jeroboam had had a *plan*. He was obeying God's overall instructions, but he didn't wait for God to give him every detail. He didn't just "turn it all over to God" and expect God to do it for him. Jeroboam worked hard and smart and the result was success.

Ultimately, God fulfilled his promise and blessed Jeroboam with victory and the kingship. Jeroboam didn't just accept failure, nor did he see it as a closed door. Jeroboam knew that closed doors sometimes mean that God wants you to go in through the window, or even to break the door down. Instead of stopping, Jeroboam knocked down the door and sought another avenue, which God provided. Jeroboam was flexible and had another plan after the first did not work out, and he worked with his innate capabilities in order to make his second plan a success. God's promises are certain as shown in his faithfulness to David but frequently patience, persistence, and hard work are necessary on the part of his people.

Due to Jeroboam's effort, and Rehoboam's bad judgment, the plans worked out and Jeroboam was brought before the assembly of all the tribes of Israel and made king, according to God's intent. God's plan even extended to the protection of the new nation when he sent a prophet to Rehoboam warning him not to attempt any military action against the new nation and its king, "for this thing is of me." Looking back, Jeroboam's first aborted attempt at rebellion can even be seen as a part of his eventual success, an initial dry run. It is probable that he was less than happy with what he had seen as overseer of forced labor, so his rebellion was supposed to eliminate that oppression. The tribes remembered his earlier effort on their behalf, along with his managerial and leadership abilities. They saw him as an obvious choice as their king. Overall, Jeroboam proved an administratively capable king, establishing governmental centers in traditional tribal centers, and in general seems to have gotten the kingdom of Israel off to a good start in political matters.

At some point in the history of the tradition, Jeroboam was certainly seen not only as a political champion, but also as a hero of the faith, most probably in the northern kingdom. Not only is Jeroboam presented in very sympathetic, even heroic form in the early part of his career, but there are many striking similarities between the story of Jeroboam and Moses's. In both narratives, God's chosen people are subjected to oppression in the form of involuntary labor, which Israel saw as intolerable slavery. In the Moses story, this was imposed by Pharaoh; in Jeroboam's case, by Solomon; in both, God raised up a deliverer who eventually, after a long absence, ended the subjugation.

There are many other comparisons to be made. God issued a call to Moses and to Jeroboam to take actions which would bring about the liberation of the covenant people, so both of them were called by God to the task which they completed. Both Moses and Jeroboam had begun as part of the oppression, as members of the oppressing class, Moses as adopted member of Pharaoh's daughter's family, Jeroboam as administrator of forced labor under Solomon. As such, both Moses and Jeroboam were trained and educated as administrators and leaders by the oppressors themselves, whom they ultimately turned against at God's direction. Moreover, Moses showed a distinct tendency to act instead of watch as seen in his killing of the Egyptian who had been beating a Hebrew and by his helping the daughters of Jethro when they were being bullied by herdsmen. We have seen the same tendency to act on Jeroboam's part, as when he rebelled against Solomon and when he came to the assembly at Shechem. Moses and Jeroboam also both made an initial attempt at ending the oppression and, in both cases, the first attempt was unsuccessful, causing each to flee across the Egyptian border. Moses killed the abusive Egyptian taskmaster, and Jeroboam tried to start a revolution—both of these initial attempts were disasters but resulted in the beginnings of what would become success.

As a part of the process of liberating Israel, both Moses and Jeroboam had face-to-face meetings with the oppressor King. Moses went before Pharaoh several times to demand on God's behalf that Pharaoh "let my people go," and Jeroboam and the official gathering of the tribes of Israel spoke to Rehoboam at the assembly at Shechem in I Kings 12. Because of those meetings, while God worked in the efforts of both Moses and Jeroboam, a successful liberation was set into motion in both cases. Then the oppressor king attempted a military recovery of the liberated Israel but was prevented from doing so by God. Pharaoh's chariots were overcome in the sea, and Rehoboam was told by God through the prophet Shemaiah that he should do nothing of a military nature against the newly independent tribes. Jeroboam and Moses later became the political leaders of the tribes of Israel, and both held that position for life.

In each of the men's stories we see the establishment of a new pattern of worship. Moses had the tabernacle built, and Jeroboam established new places of worship. Neither custom of worship was limited to a single place. Moses initiated a mobile tabernacle, and Jeroboam sanctioned worship centers at several geographical locations. This last similarity also points up the greatest difference between the two men: both were tested by golden calves. Moses passed his golden calf test; regrettably, Jeroboam did not.

So we see that far from being a total villain, Jeroboam had many admirable qualities which he coupled with attentiveness and obedience to God with the result that this godly servant found himself chosen by the LORD for a great work—obtaining the kingship. And because of Jeroboam's willingness to make changes in his own life and take calculated risks, God used him to accomplish the auspicious purpose for the northern tribes and the entire body of the chosen people.

The pattern of covenant, sin, redemption which we have been following is certainly present in this story. God's covenant with Israel is one of freedom, and God works to emancipate Israel from bondage of forced labor. The sin is Solomon's and consists of polytheism and oppression of Israel. God sees and judges that sin and removes the largest and wealthiest part of Israel from the Davidic kingdom. The redemption is found in the nation of Israel and Jeroboam rising up against servitude and establishing a separate kingdom with Jeroboam as king, all at God's command. The northern nation was thoroughly tribal in nature, in great contrast to Solomon's, and no mention is made in Kings of any northern monarch trying to use forced labor from Israel. In the northern kingdom's version of this story, even the high places like the temples at Bethel and Dan and the golden calves were seen as a part of the redemption and as the restoration of the true "old-time religion" of the tribes and a rejection of the new-fangled big-city ways of Jerusalem.

When I Kings moves from Jeroboam's political actions and turns to his work in the realm of what we today would call religious policies, a major change takes place. Jeroboam and his religious policies are presented in a radically different light than are his political works. In his quest for the kingship, the political liberation of Israel Jeroboam had obeyed God. In setting up the worship of God there, Jeroboam ceases his compliance with the laws and plans of God, however, and goes his own way with much less satisfactory results.

The change in Jeroboam's motives, actions, and outcomes take place when he fails General Thomas "Stonewall" Jackson's famous dictum, "Never take counsel of your fears." If you do, fear becomes your driving force instead of your goals and plans directing you. For Jeroboam, fear defeated faith, and this convinced him to follow his own plan, not God's. Prior to Jeroboam's establishment of the golden calves, he had mastered his insecurities, trusted and obeyed God, accomplished his objective. But in the realm of national worship policies, Jeroboam let his doubts get the best of him, and he ceased to do God's bidding. The upshot was not good, in fact disastrous.

Jeroboam was afraid that God's program wouldn't keep him on the throne, so he substituted his own for God's. Jeroboam feared that the belief that Jerusalem's temple was the greatest and best place of worship would cause the northern tribes to return their political loyalty to Jerusalem. By being controlled by his doubts and fears instead of his faith, Jeroboam brought about the very thing he sought to avoid: the fall of his dynasty. It was what we today would call a self-fulfilling prophecy. In short, Jeroboam had trusted God's plan to gain him the kingship, but he was doubtful that he'd keep it for him., so he devised his own plan and followed it instead of God's plan.

Jeroboam's fears were natural, normal, valid, and understandable. Being afraid was not a sin, but giving in to it was. General Jackson's "Never take counsel of your fears" axiom assumes that we will be afraid but tells us that our fears must not be our impetus. Being afraid is simply a reaction to living in a fallen world, but we must remember who is ultimately in control. Psalm 23 tells us "Yea though I walk through the valley of the shadow of death, I shall fear no evil, for thou art with me" (KJV). We are not to fear evil: we are not told that we should not be afraid of the other things in the valley at times. The valley is a dark, scary place in which we lose loved ones, feel pain, and become decrepit. There is much to fear in the valley of the shadow of death, and if you go into that valley and you're not afraid, it's not because you're trusting God—it's because you're not paying attention. But while we will be afraid intermittently, we don't have to be frightened of evil. God has defeated it, and God is in control, ultimately, eternally.

Alas, Jeroboam lost sight of that and failed God, Israel, and himself. He didn't become evil or become God's opponent, but he missed a fabulous opportunity to become one of the foremost heroes of our religious tradition. So often our sins do the same to us. They hold us back. We don't become completely evil or bad people, but we miss out on rich blessings which God tries to give us. We substitute our plan for God's, and too late we realize that God's was better all along. Jeroboam's call to Israel to "Behold your gods, O Israel" is indicative of his having followed his own path instead of God's. Almighty God prohibited such images, but Jeroboam incorporated them into a stratagem to maintain the religious loyalty of the northern tribes to his own religious establishments. His statement "Behold your gods" was in reality saying "Behold my plan." His plan had become his *god*. Whenever our plans take over, they're our gods, our golden calves, our idols. In Genesis 3, recall that the serpent told Eve, "You shall be like gods," and all sin is exactly that—our attempting to be God, to be our own gods. Jeroboam, like Eve, tried to be like a god, and like Eve, it was a catastrophe.[42]

Historical excursus on "The Sins of Jeroboam ben Nebat"
When we look at the actual sins of Jeroboam, we might be somewhat less than appalled. To see Jeroboam's religious policies from a very different perspective, we should look at those policies in the light of some other biblical passages.

First is the notion of high places. Jeroboam supported and participated in worship at high places, "on every high hill and under every green tree," as Deuteronomy puts it. While that is an exaggeration, high places were certainly widespread and much frequented, and Jeroboam made substantial contributions to their building funds. While Jeroboam supported the high places, he did not invent them, nor is he said to have established new ones. By worshiping there, Jeroboam is following a long-established tradition in Israel, a custom with a long and honored history.

Unlike Jeroboam, Samuel was a great hero of the faith, and yet he worshiped at several of the high places as well. In I Samuel 7, he offers sacrifice at Mizpah and erects a stone pillar at Ebenezer. In I Samuel 9, he blesses the sacrifice and presides over a sacrificial meal at the high place in an unnamed town, apparently Ramah. In the same chapter, he implies approval of men worshiping at Bethel and of prophetic activity at the high place at Gibeath-elohim, after which he informs Saul that he will come to Gilgal to offer sacrifice. Gilgal is also the site in chapter 11 of sacrifices at which Samuel is present, and in chapter 16, Samuel goes to Bethlehem to offer sacrifice as a part of the anointing of David as king.

In Judges 6, Gideon is commanded by the angel of the LORD to build an altar in his hometown of Ophrah, apparently on the

---

42. A similar treatment of the story of Jeroboam but with different emphasis is found in Richard D. Nelson, *First and Second Kings, Interpretation Commentary*, (Louisville, KY: John Knox Press, 1987), 71-82.

former site of an altar to Baal which Gideon is commanded to destroy, thus converting a Canaanite high place into an Israelite Yahwistic high place. God is pleased enough with Gideon's obedience to ignite the fire which consumed the offering. Likewise, Joshua builds an altar and sacrifices animals on Mount Ebal in Joshua 8, revisiting the established sanctuary near the site in Joshua 24.

While these acts of worship at high places are partly explained by I Kings 3:2 which tells us that high places were permitted only until the construction of the temple at Jerusalem, it must also be noted that in I Kings 18, Elijah offers sacrifice at Mount Carmel, which certainly qualifies as a high place, and this sacrifice takes place after the establishment of the Jerusalem temple. Elijah's sacrifice is obviously approved by God. Clearly at certain times, high places were legitimately seen to be holy and proper for worship and sacrifice. Great pillars of the faith worshiped at lots of those shrines without censure and with God's express permission.

In another of his practices, Jeroboam ordained priests who were not Levites, but that had been done before. The best known of these non-Levitical clergy would be none other than Samuel, who was not a Levite but an Ephraimite. Still, he was a priest, offering sacrifices at the high places on every high hill and under every green tree, so to speak (after having apprenticed under the Levite Eli). Second Samuel 8:18 tells us that David's sons were priests even though they certainly were not hereditary Levites. Also Elijah functions as a priest at Mount Carmel in I Kings 18. Priesthood in tribal religion was open to non-Levites, although Levites were thought to be superior, as seen in Judges 17 where Micah preferred a Levite priest to a homegrown one. Though Levites were top-grade priests, non-Levites were acceptable as priests at times.

Also one of Jeroboam's promulgated rituals, using icons which were prohibited by Deuteronomistic standards was done by orthodox Israelites. Samuel's rock pillar, called Ebenezer in I Samuel 7, has already been mentioned. Jacob's pillar at Bethel in Genesis 28 is another example. David in I Samuel 20 had a household religious image called a teraphim which his wife Michal put in his bed, and Saul's messengers thought it was David!

The two cherubs on the mercy seat of the ark of the covenant are perfectly acceptable representations of some characteristics of God. The cherubs there were not the fat, winged babies of medieval depiction, but huge, fierce creatures with the body of a lion, the wings of an eagle, and the head of a man. Cherubs were common religious artifacts throughout the ancient Near East during the Old Testament period, which mitigates against the denunciation of the calves because of their pagan connections. The cherubs are best seen as representations of characteristics of God: the lion's body represents strength (omnipotence), the wings represent mobility (omnipresence), and the human head represents knowledge and wisdom (omniscience). In the same manner, the bull images established by Jeroboam also represent qualities of God: strength (bulls are very strong), protectiveness (bulls protect their herd), and creator (the head bull fathers most of the calves in the herd).

A possibility for why the golden calves were a problem while cherubs were not is that bulls were used as images in Canaanite polytheistic worship, and some Israelites might become uncertain as to which god was being represented, although cherubs were an element of Canaanite worship, too. Another is that cherubs are heavenly beings while bulls are earthly. The procreative aspect of the bull image is also uncomfortably close to Canaanite fertility theology, which sees Baal bringing prosperity through divine sexual congress. Since Israel had a recurrent problem with Baal worship, ritual elements which were too similar to Canaanite idolatry and theological concepts were prohibited, eventually.

So Jeroboam's golden bull calves, while problematic, were seen by his constituents as appropriate Yahwistic icons, holy to

Yahweh the God of Israel and representing characteristics of him. These objects and images were firmly in line with the standards of tribal Yahwism as practiced by Samuel, David, and Elijah. It is probably instructive to notice that the bronze water basin in the Jerusalem temple was mounted on the backs of twelve bronze bulls (which were no longer there when the Deuteronomists did their work, having been removed by Ahaz [II Kings 16], so the Deuteronomists probably did not directly experience bulls in the Jerusalem temple).

These factors place Jeroboam's actions in a different historical light. All of the sins which he is said to have committed were also done by others who not only were *not* denounced, but are presented as heroes of the faith. During the period of the judges, the united monarchy, and the divided kingdom, there were two forms of Israelite religion, each of which was seen as legitimate in their respective places and times. Joshua, Gideon, Samuel, and David practiced an older form of the Israelite religion, which could be labelled tribal religion. This variant featured worship at multiple local high places and allowed icons, which would later be prohibited, such as David's teraphim and Samuel's pillar. It also allowed those non-hereditary priests such as Samuel and David's sons that were discussed earlier.

In contrast to this tribal religion, we find Jerusalem Yahwism, which was firmly based on the practices of the temple of Jerusalem and the royal religious establishment, and which may have been heavily influenced by the spiritual ideas of pre-Israelite Jebusite sect. This royal religion saw Jerusalem as the only true holy place and disapproved of all other local high places. It also prohibited any images except for the cherubs on the mercy seat and believed that the only true priesthood was the Jerusalem clergy.[43] Solomon seems to have tried to impose Jerusalem's form

---

43. This is treated much more fully in R. Albertz, *A History of Israelite Religion in the Old Testament Period*, (Louisville: Westminster/John Knox, 1994), 132-138.

of Yahwism on all Israel, unsuccessfully, while Jeroboam's religious policies were aimed at restoring tribal religion, naturally, for the tribes of Israel.

So we see that in a sense, Jeroboam was simply restoring the "old time religion"—attempting to bring back what had been, not trying to be evil per se. The tribes resented Solomon's innovations, both political and religious, and this dislike led to the northern tribes breaking away from the Jerusalem establishment. (This could explain the similarities between the story of Jeroboam and the one of Moses.) To those of the northern nation who practiced the old, tribal religion and were not much in favor of Solomon's new ways, Jeroboam would have seemed like a new Moses, leading them out of bondage to the evil king and reestablishing the proper worship of Yahweh, God of Israel. It was these traditional Yahwists, the vast majority of the population of the ten northern tribes, who saw Jeroboam as a paragon of the faith as well as political hero.

Still, whatever the history of the text and tradition, the Bible tells us that Jeroboam neglected to follow God completely and so missed out on an even more substantial blessing. However, as we said, it is wrong to see him as a total scoundrel and nothing else. Admittedly, chapters 12 and 13 of I Kings emphasize Jeroboam's shortcomings in worship practice, but it must also be noted that Jeroboam's last two acts we know of concern his offering honor to a prophet and his wanting to hear the prophets' messages from God. The unnamed prophet from Judah was offered lodging and food in Jeroboam's home, even after delivering a very unwelcome message. In this matter, Jeroboam was again listening to God. Near the end of his reign, Jeroboam again consults Ahijah the prophet who delivered God's initial commission to Jeroboam and offers a gift of food to him for delivering God's message.

Another strong point in Jeroboam's favor requires a careful reading of the texts condemning his religious policies. While he is castigated by the writers of Kings for his inappropriate religious artifacts, his multiple high places, and his non-Levite priests, at no point is he even remotely accused of polytheism or of Baal worship. The writers were bitterly opposed to any official sanction of polytheism or Baal worship, and had the writers known of any such acts by Jeroboam, they would surely have highlighted that sin. Since no such behaviors are recounted, it is probable that he committed none. Even Jeroboam's statement at the dedication of the golden calves, "Behold your gods, O Israel who brought you out of the land of Egypt," is probably a slight misquote of what was likely a standard liturgical refrain in the north, "Behold your God, O Israel." Jeroboam was dedicating the bulls to Israel's God who freed them from bondage.[44] Even to his detractors, Jeroboam was a committed follower of Yahweh the God of Israel, exclusively.

Another point we see in the story of Jeroboam, like we've seen in the narratives before, is that sin has consequences, and those consequences often reach far beyond the sinner to have bearing on many other people. Jeroboam set a pattern which was to be a problem for the northern kingdom throughout its existence and which was a contributing factor in its final downfall, along with Baal worship and polytheism.

---

44. The difference is a single consonant in the verb changing *they who brought you out* (plural verb) to *"he who brought you out"* (singular verb). The subject of the verb is *elohim* (in construct form with suffix [*eloheyka*]), which can be read as either plural (*your gods*) or singular (*your God*), with the singular reading of the plural word being generally reserved for Yahweh. Such a minor modification of a source in order to make a theological point is quite in keeping with biblical practice. Chron. made many such miniscule adjustments and much greater ones to its source in the books of Kings. The authors of the books of Matt and Luke treated Mark's gospel similarly. R. Albertz, *A History of Israelite Religion in the Old Testament Period* (Louisville: Westminster/John Knox,1994), 144–146.

If all of this seems to be presenting an ambivalent portrait of Jeroboam, that is exactly what the Bible does. If he was not a plaster saint with a glow-in-the-dark halo, neither was he an unmitigated villain. He was instead a human being, a person with a mixture of good and bad, obedience and disobedience, moments of greatness and moments of failure. Multidimensional, he was like all humans in that regard. He was one through whom God worked to bring about an important part of the chosen people's history in order to introduce salvation.

So if Jeroboam has so many good qualities and achieved some great things for God and was even a hero of the faith to some, why is he presented in such negative terms with his religious policies so terrible? The answer for that will have to wait until we have examined the story of Josiah, who is in many ways the opposite of Jeroboam and in the eyes of the writers of Kings, the greatest king after David.

Josiah the Reformer

Josiah is a noteworthy king and embodiment of Israelite belief who deserves greater recognition. He is a rarity, a king to whom the Deuteronomistic history gives unqualified approval. "And he did that which was right in the sight of the LORD, and walked in all the way of David his father," says II Kings 22:2 of Josiah. This king did that which was right, and the first praiseworthy thing he did, of which we are told, is to properly care for Jerusalem's temple of the LORD of Hosts and for its priesthood. In the Deuteronomistic history as a whole, the proper reverence, maintenance, and support of that temple and priesthood are major matters.[45]

---

45. The Deuteronomistic history consists of Josh., Judg., I & II Sam., and I & II Kings. It is thought by some to have been completed by editing older materials into a connected treatise in two stages. The first rendition was probably completed during the reign of Josiah and was intended to support the reform he enacted. A revision of that first draft was finished during the Babylonian Exile and was intended to explain why Israel and Jerusalem were defeated. Martin Noth's *The Deuteronomistic History* is the classic presentation of this idea, with Frank M. Cross's, *Canaanite Myth and Hebrew Epic* being a substantial revision of Noth's hypothesis. Richard Nelson in *I & II Kings: Interpretation Commentary* and in *The Historical Books* further develops this theory.

The Old Testament is vitally interested in the appropriate worship of God and the correct structuring and function of the institutions of temple and priesthood. This concern can be accounted for historically by the fact that the major sections of the Old Testament were collected, edited, and finalized by the priests, primarily the priests of Jerusalem. All of the Old Testament is not the *work* of these priests, but all of the Old Testament had to meet the *approval* of the priests in Jerusalem, who had the final say on what was included in the Scriptures. Since they were extremely interested in the temple and in ritual, such things play a prominent role in these manuscripts.

In a less historiographical, more theological vein, we see that the Bible instructs us to take worship seriously and to make a very great effort to worship God correctly, properly, and in keeping with biblical principles. We have seen in Exodus 24 that the Old Testament law regarding worship is less strictly prescriptive and definitive about worship forms than is often thought and that God did not dictate to Israel or the church a single approach to worship. There is plenty of room among the biblical guidelines and theories of worship for regional, cultural, personal, and even theological differences. We have also noticed and will see very definitely in the upcoming Josiah texts specifically that there are very definite principles which are prescriptive——however loosely—and going beyond those principles is a serious error. A key element in Josiah's reform was his efforts to seek the presence of God and ensure that his people did the same through worship that was carried out in a dignified manner, in accordance with the book of the law, the Scriptures.

The temple building and grounds are another primary concern of the priests, as the objective of the properly maintained and attended sanctuary was the presence of God among the whole group of people, not just among the priests. In 23:2–3, we see that Josiah and Hilkiah's work on the temple was culminated in a gathering of "all the people, both small and great." In the view of the reformers and of the writers of Kings, the temple was God's house and his environment for everyone. Worship is God's invitation to his people to come before him, and all of his people are clearly instructed to accept that invitation graciously. So an important piece of Josiah's reform was to take proper care of the temple structure, which was the institutional carrier of that togetherness. Prominent in Old Testament theology is God's command for the upkeep of his house and of those who are chosen and ordained to work in it, making such care and maintenance a visible sign of righteousness and devotion to God (and all God's preachers said, "Amen!").

Even before he began his restructuring, Josiah began a major repair and maintenance initiative on the temple. Very few details are given in II Kings 22, but the list of work and materials is an impressive one, so the effort was not minor or halfhearted. Josiah and the high priest Hilkiah were wanting the temple fixed, and they committed themselves to that task, but as is often the case, an action leads to completely unforeseen and unintended consequences. Josiah and Hilkiah wanted the temple restored, and they succeeded, but God had additional plans for their project. In the process of repairing and refurbishing the temple, a book was found which when unrolled and read turned out to be the "book of the law." For Josiah and Hilkiah, their faithfulness and diligence in one area of service led to opportunities for growth in other areas as well. The renovation of the temple building led to the discovery of the Word of God, which in turn led Josiah on to even greater achievements than he had anticipated. Josiah found that growth in God has many aspects which can be and usually are mutually reinforcing. Progress in one area strengthens and assists other areas. Josiah began with a physical remodeling of the temple building, but by branching out as the chance arose, he ended up changing the entire religious life of the chosen people. God was taking the longer and greater view and was working toward a much larger goal than the temple building. And for that,

God was not to be satisfied with anything less than Josiah's total commitment. God does not want to be the center of his people's religion—he demands to be the center of their entire life. Josiah took the first step, and by being attentive to further possibilities, he accomplished much for God.

The book of the law which was found was apparently an old book that had been forgotten or at least neglected. Abandonment of Scripture always leads to trouble. Probably, Manasseh's disastrous reign and relapse into polytheism came during this time of the neglect of God's word. Deuteronomy is explicit that ignoring the law and commandments leads to suffering while obedience brings blessing. The northern kingdom in Israel had disregarded the commandments and been conquered by Assyria. Similarly, Judah had neglected the book of the law and been reduced by Babylon to effectively a small city-state.

A crucial component of Josiah's great and effective reform was a simple one: Josiah and Shaphan read the book of the law. They read Scripture. They didn't just respect it, they didn't just talk about it, and they didn't just listen to other people talk about it. They didn't plan to read it someday; they didn't wait for the movie to come out. They read it. They knew firsthand what it said. And having known it so intimately, they considered what it said, and obeyed it. Reading and knowing the scripture transformed them dramatically and molded the direction of their lives. They not only read and heard the Scripture, they *acted* on what they heard. As James 1:22 says, in effect, why look in the mirror if you don't comb your hair while you're looking? Josiah was grieved by his and Judah's failure to follow the law, and he expressed his emotion by tearing his clothes. His regret and subsequent behavior were a good start but insufficient in themselves. Josiah did what knowing God and knowing Scripture should make a person do: he modified his behavior and his life, making obedience a regular daily practice. By familiarizing himself with Scripture and being changed by it, Josiah structured his life differently from then on and worked to bring it into accord with Scriptural teaching. For Israel, God's law was a major element in the covenant between God and Israel. Josiah took the covenant seriously and made a serious attempt to obey its law as set out in scripture.

Josiah, Hilkiah, and Shaphan were all, admittedly, novices at Scriptural interpretation, so Josiah sought help in understanding what he had first heard in the book of the law. He followed the biblical injunction "Trust in the LORD with all your heart, and do not rely on your own insight" (Proverbs 3:5). The assistance sought by Josiah was culturally conditioned and for his situation appropriate. He sought out the pronouncement of a prophetess of the LORD. Other cultures would find other types of decrees and messages helpful. Priests, pastors, scholars, books, preaching, Sunday school lessons, and several other types of resources for understanding Scripture were and are available to people in various places and times. They are not all equally valuable, however. Some are wonderfully helpful, others less so; some are wrong, some badly so. The best way to know which is which is to develop broad experience in using them. These types of assistance are not a replacement or a substitute for knowledge gleaned from reading and studying the Bible oneself, but they can be an excellent complement to Bible reading and reinforce the Bible's meaning.

Huldah's prophetic response is highly reminiscent of several other prophetic pronouncements in its denunciation of polytheism and its forecasting of punitive destruction. Her statement's essential theological basis is the standard religious program of the Deuteronomistic history and of Deuteronomy, all of which are very similar in many ways to the prophecies of Jeremiah. It is widely thought that there is a literary connection among all of these. The Deuteronomistic history is an analysis and evaluation of the ancient times of Israel from the perspective of the theological requirements of the book of Deuteronomy. This book is widely thought to have been the "book of the law" found in the temple during Josiah's renovations and therefore is an important basis of his religious and political reforms. The book of Jeremiah shares much of the theological ideas and language of the Deuteronomistic history.[46]

Huldah's message contains three points, which will be examined here. First, she validated Scripture as documents connecting us to God. Her statement that God was about to invoke the curse clause of the scroll was not welcome news. But it certainly gave the prophetic stamp of approval to the book as the true word of God, which Josiah could trust. Her authentication of the curses also has a happier note. If the curses were true, then the blessings were true, and God's people could rely on them as well.

A second point she makes is that sustained belief in God and the exclusive worship of him are requirements that cannot be skirted. Israel had failed to practice that exclusive worship, and their military defeat and economic hardships stemmed from that lack of faithfulness. Israel was tempted by idolatry and polytheism and had fallen into them too often. Again we see the biblical principle that God sees sin and judges it. Denunciation and prohibition of polytheism are major themes of Deuteronomy and of the Deuteronomistic history. In fact, it is the leading theme of the story of Josiah. The imagery of fire in Huldah's statement that due to Israel's polytheism God's wrath will be kindled and not quenched is found in other biblical texts and in several of the others has a dual meaning of punishment and redemption. In Isaiah 1:31, God threatens Israel with fiery destruction, but in Isaiah 1:25, the fire is the refiner's fire which purifies Israel; the fire will remove Israel's iniquity, and the burning is the means of purification and restoration as well as punishment. A nearly identical image is found in Malachi 3:2-3. Isaiah 6 provides an important clue about God's cleansing fire. Isaiah confesses his

---

46. John Bright, *A History of Israel* (Philadelphia: Westminster, 1972), 295, 318; Martin Noth, *The History of Israel* (New York: Harper and Row, 1960), 275.

sin of unclean lips and recognizes that his sin makes him unworthy to come before the LORD, but the angel takes a coal from the altar where sacrifice is burned and touches Isaiah's mouth, taking away his guilt and bringing atonement through the fire of the sacrifice. Again we see sacrifice as the means of bringing forgiveness.

King Josiah and the priest Hilkiah have seen to the care of the temple, found the book of the law, read it, and had it authenticated by a prophet. So Josiah takes the obvious next step of putting the commandments of the law into effect. But before Josiah begins issuing orders and instructions regarding the law, he takes a very sensible and practical first step of building support for the project among the people of his kingdom. As king, Josiah had to be a politician, and since his role as king included a part in the spiritual culture of Israel, his political responsibilities extended into the religious realm as well. In fact, Israel didn't see any separation between its political life and its religious life. Both were under the control of Yahweh as part of the covenant, and God was as interested and involved in Israel's social, legal, economic, and military affairs as in its piety. As we've said, God doesn't want his people to obey him just in religious things; he wants them to obey him in *all* things.

So Josiah begins his reform with a ceremony intended to secure the assent, cooperation, and participation of his entire kingdom. The list of participants in the covenant ceremony related in II Kings 23:1–3 is an impressive one: all the elders of Judah and Jerusalem, all the men of Judah, and in fact all the inhabitants of Jerusalem—the priests, the prophets, and the regular citizens, both great and small. The lowest peasant and the highest ranks were all included in the proceedings. The earthly distinctions among humans had no impact on whether the person was bound by God's law and included in the covenant. God is no respecter of persons, and he is as interested in the average people of the land as in the kings, nobles, and priests. It's hard to imagine who was left out of this list and this landmark event. But an important point about this assembly is that it was not primarily a political meeting but a worship service held in the temple, the house of God. It was God's people coming together to be with him. Josiah and Judah sought to obey God's laws, and as a first step they sought God's presence in formal, corporate worship.

The key to the covenant ceremony was the commitment by all involved to keep the law of God with all their heart and soul. This made the idea more than a promise to modify their behavior. It would reach down into their actual thoughts and attitudes and bring them into conformance with God's intentions. The people committed to obeying the spirit of the law as well as the letter. Many references in the Bible speak of the need to align one's attitudes as well as external actions with God and condemn sterile, tone-deaf actions without the appropriate motivations and intentions. Isaiah 1:10–20; Hosea 4:12–14 and 8:11; Amos 4:4–5 and 5:4–6; and Matthew 7:21 all address this issue in showing how much the writers despise the approach that sees token performance as equivalent to faithfulness. Josiah and Judah were intent on avoiding this mistake and promised to adjust their hearts and souls as well as their rituals.

The covenant element in the story of Josiah has two tracks. One involves formal worship and is manifested in the national covenant ceremony which Josiah called. The other is farther reaching and requires more long-term, individual dedication. After the communal expression, Josiah and Israel put their promise into effect and cleaned up their worship and their moral lives. So the recurrent themes of covenant, sin, redemption are very evident in this story once again.

It is interesting to note that according to the chronology of II Kings 23, Josiah is making the covenant to obey God and the book of the law at the same time that in the temple right behind him there are still altars and vessels holy to Baal and the host of heaven. Here we have a very practical biblical application of the principle that the proper sequence is not to get your life straightened out and then turn to God, but rather to turn to God, who will then help you get yourself righted around. Josiah committed himself to the LORD and *then* started cleaning the sin out. So he was able to successfully eliminate the polytheism from the temple and the official, orthodox religion of Israel. As we saw in the garden of Eden with the fig leaves, human attempts to clean up sin don't work but God can get it done if we accept his offer of atonement.

The covenant ceremony in Kings is rather highly reminiscent of the one at Mount Sinai related in Exodus 19–24. In both, the chosen people gather at a holy place, and before God they promise to obey his decrees. In both, a mediator goes up to God and leads the people in their promise—Moses to the mountaintop and Josiah to the temple pillars. Pillars play a role at Sinai as well (Exodus 24:4). In both, the law is read to the people, and all the people assent to the covenant.

So now with the statutes in hand and the covenant ceremony in which they were promising to obey them, and all the people supporting the reform effort, the hard labor begins. The actual business of daily life in keeping with the covenant is quite different from the ceremony and the theoretical part—as every married couple finds out very quickly. The excitement of the wedding gives way to the mundane realities of work, car payments, dirty dishes, crying babies, and argumentative teenagers. Likewise, the excitement of the covenant ceremony gave way to the reality of a nation and people in a mess with idols, wrong religious practices, and an awful lot of work to do to make it right. But like in a marriage where love, determination, and hard work get you through, Josiah and Judah pledged to be devoted to the LORD, serve him conscientiously, and put the law into strict effect.

In all such large endeavors, establishing priorities is necessary, and the first in Deuteronomy and in II Kings 23 was the elimination of polytheism from Israel. Elijah quite colorfully asked Israel, "How long will you go limping with two different opinions?" The Bible presents a rigid and stark choice: God is the only God, or he isn't God at all. Worship him alone, or you reject him completely. God is not the high God among many gods; he is not the father of the gods. He is the *only* God.

The elimination of Baal worship was the first priority of Josiah's sweeping renovation of the nation's temple and faith. Devotion to that god was a particularly pernicious sin for Israel because its promise of economic well-being through ceremonial sex with the Canaanite temple priests and priestesses. The root temptation of Baal worship which drew Israel in was sex-saturated materialism. (As Koheleth says in Ecclesiastes, "There is nothing new under the sun.")

The extermination of Baal worship and polytheism was radical and thorough. Every wrong and questionable practice connected with Baal worship was eliminated. Antiquity and tradition were no protection. The respected origin of the high places was not sufficient to keep them. "We've always done it that way!" was not a valid reason to continue, a fallacy. Some traditions are traditional mistakes. "It's been that way for thirty years" sometimes means that God has spent thirty years trying to get it changed. Josiah and Hilkiah were determined to annihilate belief in multiple gods, and they made a mighty and determined effort to remove it completely from Israel. They were effectively burning their bridges behind them so that there was no going back. From Baal Peor in Numbers 25, to Elijah's contest with the Baal prophets in I Kings 18, to Jeremiah's day, Baal worship was a frequent sin in Israel and Josiah was resolved to get rid of it for all time. Sin was clearly evident in the need for the cleansing of the temple and the high places in this chapter as well as in the need to make major personnel changes in the priesthood.

A central idea of Deuteronomy and the Deuteronomistic history is that God is holy and he demands holiness from his people. Their polytheism and sexual sins in pursuit of Baal's false promise of prosperity prevented Israel being the holy people it should be, so God commanded that extreme measures be taken to get rid of the polytheism. A holy people must render holy worship, and what had been going on at the Baal shrines was very far from holy. God doesn't demand uniformity of worship practices of his modern church like he did of Israel, but he demands unity of heart, a holy people united in love of God and love of his people. Sacred prostitution no less than commercial prostitution sees other people as objects to be used for one's own pleasure and benefit, and such a mindset is not in keeping with God's commandment to love your neighbor as yourself.

Josiah's reform was not clearing the speck out of his neighbor's eye. As we see in verses 4 and 6–7, he began with his own house and the royal temple in Jerusalem because he was aware that it was as much in need of correction as any other. He didn't just demand that other people change their ways—he began by addressing the errors of his own establishment and his own house. Josiah started his restoration by cleaning up his own surroundings in an expanding circle: the temple, his own city, his own kingdom, and then his nation. He obeyed Matthew 7:3–5 by getting the beam out of his own eye first.

That the problems of Baal worship and polytheism had infected every part of Israelite life is shown by its presence in the temple of Jerusalem. Abominable acts were being carried out in the place where God's holiness should have been the most venerated. The priests seem to have enthusiastically participated in the cleansing of the temple, though, and took all the artifacts which were associated with the worship of other gods out of the temple, burned them down in the garbage dump, and scattered the ashes on graves, completely desecrating the former sacred pole. The residue of the vessels was taken to Bethel, probably for the purpose of desecrating both the vessels and the idolatrous altar at Bethel.

While Josiah started with his own mess, his reform went far beyond that and included all of the nation. With his own immediate house now in order, Josiah tackles the slightly more distant problem of the high places which had become infected with polytheism. In verse 5, idolatrous priests connected with polytheism were deposed from their positions as clergy and forced to find other means of livelihood. This firing of priests was a part of Josiah's cleaning out of his own government. These high places and priests had been established by the kings of Judah and were at least sanctioned by the royal establishment and probably supported by it as well. But they were not royal shrines and were positioned throughout the cities of Judah, not just in Jerusalem.

Next, Josiah tackles the problem of the high places which are devoted to Yahweh but whose priests are not identified as idolatrous or as polytheistic and are therefore legitimate priests in illegitimate shrines. If, as is likely, these priests were Levites, Deuteronomy 18 tells that they lived in towns throughout Israel but prescribes that these country priests should be allowed to come to the single legitimate altar and temple in Jerusalem for the purpose of offering their sacrifices there. Whatever the status of these priests, their treatment by the king is quite different from the priests who had been identified as idolatrous. The idolatrous polytheistic priests were let go and forced to find honest work, but in striking contrast, the legitimate priests retained their status as clergy. This is seen by the statement in verse 9 that "they ate unleavened bread among their brethren." Unleavened bread was used in worship rituals as seen in 23:18 and Leviticus 2:11, 6:17, 7:13, and 23:17 and was especially associated with Passover. Apparently, these local priests, who were probably Levites, retained their functions as local clergy and still conducted ceremonies in which unleavened bread was a prominent feature, but they lost their sacrificial rights.

It may be significant to note that these priests are not reported to have been idolatrous or polytheistic. Certainly, many in

Israel were faithful to the one true God and kept the true faith in the face of pressures to relent. But too many Israelites, including many of the priests, did not remain faithful and began again to worship other gods. The problem of the Israelite people was in going along with the culture of the time. The culture said, "Worshiping God is okay, but you've got to have Baal, Asherah, and fertility, too." Instead of standing firmly for the truth of the one true God, too many Israelites just went along. They said, "I can still worship God—still keep his covenant while worshiping Baal and assuring prosperity for myself."

While in scholarly circles we call that process syncretism, it really was compromising with evil. It wasn't "get along, go along." It wasn't accommodating diversity. It was sin. It was denying the truth of God. It was worshiping things instead of God. This was why the best of the Israelite religious leaders were unequivocal in their denunciations of the popular religion which mingled Baal worship with the worship of Yahweh. For example, and there are many, there is: Elijah crying out "How long will you limp along of two minds?" (I Kings 18:21 [author's translation]); Hosea preaching that "Ephraim is joined to idols, leave him alone" (Hosea 4:17); the prophets and Levites calling Israel to the exclusive worship of the true God; Josiah calling the people to obey the book of the law; and the writer of Kings condemning the "idolatrous priests" of the high places who allowed their sacred precincts to become infiltrated and contaminated by the practices and thoughts of the prevailing materialistic, sex-saturated culture around them. These men stood true to God against the prevailing tide of compromise, of silence in the face of wrong. They, and others who were on the LORD's side, held fast in the true faith and in obedience.

But they were too few. Too many were "of two minds" and unwilling to resist the siren calls of unbridled sexuality, good times, and wealth. Such an attitude even had infected the highest levels of the faith. Even the old mainline temples were the scenes of

Baal rituals. Josiah was radical in his reaction of shutting them down and defiling them, but such a drastic measure was necessary by that time of such an advanced state of corruption. Even though it was too little, too late to prevent the downfall of the kingdom, after this time we hear no more of official Israelite religion engaging in such syncretistic practices.

So in a very real sense, Josiah's changes to Israel's theology and ritual were highly effective. It made a permanent change in way the official religion was practiced. While some polytheistic practices held on longer in popular religion (Jeremiah 44:14–19; Ezekiel 8:14), the orthodox Israelite procedures were made permanently monotheistic. The prophesied failure of Josiah's attempt to prevent the destruction of the kingdom did not prevent Josiah giving it his best shot. Josiah and his fellow reformers were determined to sincerely, adamantly obey the book of the law and the commandment to "have no other gods before me."

The reform did not stop with ritual matters, but had a definite staunch moral element as well. Besides sacred prostitution being banned, child sacrifice was also eliminated from Israel's worship. Such nefarious worship practices were prohibited. Bethel came in for especially severe treatment from the reformers. But much more extreme, the priests at Bethel were not deposed—they were killed. The reason for this severity of approach at Bethel may be explained by II Kings 17 where Bethel was made into a shrine of "the god of the land" who had sent lions among the foreign peoples settled in the area by the Assyrians. These pagan peoples had continued to worship their own gods but wanted to placate "the god of the land" as well so he would call off his lions. So this religion at Bethel employed not the worship of Yahweh established by Jeroboam, but was a syncretistic cult, thoroughly polytheistic, and in which Yahweh was not the high God but one god among many. He was simply the god of the local area. The worshipers at Bethel didn't see Yahweh as the only or even highest god of all, but simply as the local lion god. The Assyrian-sponsored cult had reduced Yahweh to a minor local deity, and our "jealous" God wanted that view totally destroyed, discredited, and obliterated past recovery. Therefore Josiah took drastic steps to end that heretical perversion.

While the reform led by Josiah and Hilkiah was, like all human endeavors, less than perfect, it made some important, far-reaching and radical changes in Israel. The concept of a written Scripture as a permanent, fixed guide to belief and practice also remained as an integral part of the worship of God by his people. Josiah did not see the full effect of his efforts, but he sowed some very good seed which is still being harvested. He was presented as a great king because of his remarkable adherence to his upright values. He conformed his acts as king to the law of God, intentionally, thoroughly, and with precision—and apparently wholeheartedly and with enthusiasm. While some of it was not very pretty or pleasant, Josiah stayed with it. Such radical obedience is commanded and demanded by God, and nothing less is acceptable.

When Josiah began his work, he was not in a situation which seemed to be advantageous for someone whose goal was to change the whole world. Josiah was king over only a small town and its associated farmlands. Jerusalem was not particularly wealthy and possessed neither highly fertile lands nor rich trade routes. It had no exploitable natural resources aside from its agricultural base and quarries. What it had was the temple and a king and high priest who were determined to do what they could for God and the work of the kingdom of God. Through this dedication of the part of Josiah, Hilkiah, and their followers, God wiped the slate clean. This is the redemption which God effected through the events in this story.

Josiah had very little, but what he did have he gave to God, and, like when Jesus fed five thousand with the boy's lunch, God took what Josiah had and made something great out of it. Josiah was not able to permanently rebuild the united kingdom of Israel and Judah. He didn't make Israel safe and secure. His apparent political goals were not met. But God used Josiah's reform to change much of the world. Since the time of Josiah, all biblical religions have been thoroughly Josianic. Deuteronomy is still accounted as Scripture. The idea of monotheism has become the dominant religious concept in western religion. The core religious doctrines written down and publicly acknowledged as the divine Scriptural standard are still an essential element of all biblically based faiths.

Josiah and Jeroboam

Jeroboam was a hero of the faith in one sense and yet ultimately is seen in Scripture as a failure. He was true to Yahweh and was not polytheistic. He was a fervent, dedicated worshiper of God and a major financial contributor. He supported the building fund and the clergy. But he led Israel in a direction counter to that in which God wanted. Jeroboam was trying to take Israel back to the old ways when God was trying to take them into new ways. First Kings clearly says that Jeroboam's problem from a Scriptural point of view was his decision not to recognize the primacy of Jerusalem. While that is in some sense anachronistic (Jerusalem wasn't a national temple at the time, but a royal shrine, in other words riff-raff *not* welcome), Jeroboam's religious program supported the local aspect of sacrifice and continued the practice just about everywhere. This reinforced animal sacrifice of as a central part of everyone's regular worship. God's plan was the centralization of worship in one place with sacrifice being offered *on behalf* of everyone but not being offered *by* everyone. This centralized sacrificial system retained the act as a prime part of the national religion but rendered it a much less integral part of local and personal worship. Josiah brought this plan to fruition when he brought together all sacrifice in Jerusalem.

After Josiah, sacrifice was no longer the main centerpiece of regular worship; it was not even a normal part of most Israelites' experience. After Josiah, for most orthodox Israelites, sacrifice was something the priests did in a faraway place which most Israelites seldom or never saw. With Josiah's reform in place based on Deuteronomy, sacrifice was mostly gone from local ritual. Sacrifice was no longer the centerpiece of the covenant in the eyes of Israelite villagers. Instead, right living, in accordance with the laws of God, was paramount to being a follower of God.

When the Babylonians destroyed Jerusalem, Israel as a whole in a religious sense barely noticed the loss of the temple and sacrifice. For two generations, sacrifice had not been an important part of their everyday lives or of their regular worship, and therefore the lack of sacrifice being offered was not a death blow to their covenant with God. The loss was important to them, but not in the sense that their covenant, their faith, or their religion could not survive. Regular worship was centered on preaching and prayer, not sacrifice. Moreover, when the temple was restored under Aaronide control, it was still a distant reality to most Jews. Sacrifice was necessary for the forgiveness of sin, but those offerings were something which was being done by someone else far away. Daily life in the covenant was much more wrapped up in household ritual and Sabbath, and daily living rightly according to the dictates of Scripture. So it is interesting to note that through the work of Josiah and his supporters God had prepared Israel to be his people even without regular animal sacrifice. His people could continue as the chosen covenant people of God, even without the temple or blood offerings.

The Christian connotations are clear and similar. Those offered by the high priest and his Aaronide colleagues were on behalf of everyone and were thought to be effective for all Israel. In the same way, Jesus's death was a sacrifice for every single human being and was eternally efficacious for all who believe. The

Christian concept of Jesus' atoning death for all humanity was built on groundwork laid by Josiah and Deuteronomy.

The Deuteronomistic reform under Josiah conceived of sacrifice as a cosmic event very unlike the older tradition of every family offering sacrifice in their own village. Therefore, Jeroboam's work, while well intentioned and firmly grounded in the traditions of the fathers, was at odds with God's plans for his people. Jeroboam was not a bad man, and his actions were not intentional rebellion against God—in fact, quite the opposite. But his intentions did not make up for being insufficiently attentive to God's instructions. Jeroboam was afraid of losing his own power and authority and let that fear lead him into a mistake, and this sabotaged him. It was a well-intentioned error, but still an error.

This is probably why Jeroboam receives such disapproval from the writers of Kings. Kings is part of the Deuteronomistic history, which is generally thought to have been compiled in support of Josiah's reform as presented in II Kings 23. Jeroboam was in many ways the anti-Josiah, and their programs of worship were essentially diametrical opposites within the confines of orthodox Yahwism. So for the writers of Kings, Jeroboam represented what was wrong with Israel, and Josiah represented what was right about it. Even though that judgment is applying the standards of a later time and a little unfair to Jeroboam, it reflects the direction in which God was leading Israel—a direction which Josiah followed but Jeroboam did not.

Have Mercy on Me, O God

An important principle of interpreting the Bible is that stories about people who err and sin are not put there for us to see how bad they were and conversely feel good about ourselves because we haven't done that particular sin. These stories show us our own sin because we commit sins of the same categories. Of course, we don't worship Baal, but we certainly fall into materialism and sexual sin, even if only in our minds. Notwithstanding, it's very tempting and understandable to read about Manasseh and say, "Ooh, wasn't he bad?"

The list of his sins is a long and exhaustive—and exhausting—one. Polytheism and human sacrifice are the core sins, but Manasseh didn't stop with those sins. He also "practiced soothsaying and augury and sorcery, and dealt with mediums and with wizards" (verse 6), all of which were specifically prohibited by Deuteronomy. He also committed ritual sins by rebuilding high places and putting up illegitimate altars and images in the Jerusalem temple. Chronicles may be understating the case when it says, "He did much evil in the sight of the LORD, provoking him to anger" (verse 6). As if those sins weren't enough, Manasseh seduced the people of Judah and Jerusalem to commit those sins, too.

Another caveat to remember in interpreting Bible stories is that the sinner in the story didn't wake up in the morning and think, "What can I do to disobey God today?" But I can't help but think that in this case King Manasseh might have done exactly that.

An important point in the whole Bible which is a key element in Israel's covenant with God is evident in this story. As we have seen time and time again, God sees sin, God judges sin, and God punishes sin. In addition, God is willing to forgive sin, but by no means does that indicate that he doesn't care about sin. God gives us freedom to make our own choices, but that independence does not mean that wrong choices don't matter or that they don't have further effects. God takes sin seriously, and he responds to our sin.

Manasseh and Judah had available to them the knowledge they needed in order to make good decisions and to do right. They had some form of the law—God's teachings and ordinances—which clearly forbade the sinful practices that Manasseh and Judah committed. The laws, statutes, and regulations existed prior to Manasseh's sins, and he should have consulted the teachings, learned them, and been guided by them. Verse 10 states that while the sins were going on, God spoke to Manasseh and Judah, but they wouldn't listen. What means that God used to speak to them isn't specified, whether prophets, whirlwind, or priest, but he communicated. Manasseh and Judah, unfortunately, wouldn't pay attention.

That was bad, but again, we shouldn't just think about how bad Manasseh was. Very often, we current-day Christians commit sins which are clearly against God's will as set forth in Scripture. We read the Bible text and then explain the prohibition away. Too many Christians seem to think that if it's trendy, it isn't sin. That's faulty thinking. Some sins have always been trendy and they've still been sins. Baal worship was that way. Sexual sin is always in style in some circles, but those circles shouldn't include the church.

A convincing example of the covenant principle that God judges and punishes sin is found in the notice in verse 11 that God sent the Assyrian army to capture Manasseh and take him as a prisoner to Babylon. This points to the biggest critical question regarding the story of Manasseh. Second Kings does not mention Manasseh's imprisonment, nor his repentance and restoration. The historical uncertainty regarding the veracity of the chroniclers' account of Manasseh's repentance versus the Deuteronomistic silence about it is closely connected with the theological perspectives and themes of the two works.

The Deuteronomists see Manasseh as primarily responsible for the fall of Jerusalem and the subsequent exile. So they have no interest in recounting a story in which Manasseh is forgiven and reinstated. Obviously, such redemption would seem to negate the Deuteronomistic assignment of blame to Manasseh. On the other hand, the chroniclers, knowing of the return from Exile and reconstruction of the temple and Jerusalem, are much less interested in assigning responsibility for the end of the kingdom and more eager to relate how the post-exilic community needs to adopt proper worship practices and stay faithful to the covenant. In their view, Manasseh's cycle of captivity, repentance, and restoration is a wonderful example of how God works to bring redemption to his people.

It has long been standard to accord more historical veracity to the Deuteronomistic history than to the books of Chronicles, and that judgment is probably correct. The chroniclers' clearly anachronistic accounts of the reigns of the Judaean kings, especially those of David and Solomon, show that historical accuracy is not the primary purpose of this group of writers. Instead, much of their work is seen as a retrojection of the priestly views and organization of their own day back into monarchic era temple practices. This is probably an attempt to justify the post-exilic priesthood and its processes and rules by showing them as having been instituted by David and Solomon (II Chronicles 8: 14–16). But to simply reject Chronicles as historical fantasy is much too harsh a stance. It is highly likely that the chroniclers had access to some sources which the Deuteronomists did not use, and some of these sources seem to have as much historical value as those used by the Deuteronomists.

There has been much discussion regarding the historicity of Chronicles' account of Manasseh's imprisonment, repentance, and subsequent reform efforts. Some see the whole narrative as an attempt to account for the evil Manasseh being the king of Judah with the longest reign.[47] Assyrian records do not preclude such an event since vassal kings were at times given such treatment. That such a circumstance befalling Manasseh would cause him to see the error of his ways is quite believable. That Chronicles simply invents such an episode is unlikely, but some source used by the chronicler may have done so. A main argument against the historicity of the account is that Kings makes no mention of it, nor do any Assyrian records. Even more telling is that Josiah had to eliminate several practices and installations attributed to Manasseh, so Manasseh's reform as recounted in Chronicles must have been half-hearted and incomplete at best.

Whatever the historical basis, the story of Manasseh is a transparent example of the themes of covenant, sin, and redemption, which we have been seeing in all the stories. As king of Judah, Manasseh is the recipient of the Zion/David covenant as well as the Sinai covenant with all Israel. Yet Manasseh's sins broke nearly all of the covenant stipulations.

So both works have an ideological bias and treat Manasseh in the light of that theological perspective. Arbitrary rejection of the Chronicles account is therefore overly hasty. In spite of their

---

47. See Carl Evans, "Manasseh, King of Judah," *Anchor Bible Dictionary*, vol. 4 (New York: Doubleday, 1992), 498–499 for a summary of the positions and references.

differences, both Kings and Chronicles have several theological points in common, one of which is that God judges and punishes sin

Resulting punishment is not always so direct and so obvious as happened with Manasseh. Sometimes the punishment isn't even visible, but sin has consequences. As we saw, the thematic thread of sin illustrates that frequently the penalty is simply the missed blessing that we lose because of our failure to obey.

Manasseh's sin brought a very direct punishment, although. He went from being king of Judah to being a prisoner in Babylon. At this point the story of Manasseh is quite reminiscent of the story of the prodigal son, a "riches to rags" story if you will. Both people were in a really bad situation which had been brought on by their own wrongful actions. Both were far from home and without resources. Manasseh and the prodigal son each recognized that they had sinned and that their sin had brought them to a horrible spot in life. (But then it's hard not to notice that something is wrong when you're having to wrestle with the pigs for your share of the slop!) There was that difference between their situations, though: God had intervened in Manasseh's case and dealt with it right then and there. The prodigal son, on the other hand, was suffering the natural consequences of his own stupidity. But in both cases, we see that sin hurts.

Christians today in the West do not normally face exile and arrest (although some do), nor are we forced into pig pens. But being out of God's will is spiritual exile and living a life of sin are certainly the equivalents of being trapped in a pig pen.

Manasseh had not listened very well to God's messages, but he apparently heard some of it, because he knew that repentance and prayer were the proper responses to his wrongdoing and imprisonment. Repentance is a turning around in a new direction, and Manasseh did exactly that. He modified his focus and behavior away from doing evil and was contrite. Manasseh changed from a life centered on idols to a life humbly centered on God.

In cases of true repentance, God sometimes puts aside the results of sin like he did in the case of Manasseh. But not always. David repented of his sin with Bathsheba, but the baby died anyway. A drug-addicted single mother who repents and changes is forgiven but still has two children with serious health problems. Still, in every case, God accepts the gesture and lovingly restores the apologetic sinner to his kingdom. Manasseh and the prodigal son were reintegrated into their families and sonship due to their confessions and sorrow. Manasseh prayed for forgiveness and changed his behavior. So this story is clear example of the theme of redemption. God restored Manasseh and returned him to the throne of Judah.

I suspect that most of us in Manasseh's situation, if we were in a Babylonian prison, would have made a lot of dire promises to God. Most of us have done that without being in prison! We're very good at making promises, but we're not nearly so great at keeping them. That kind of repentance is easy but less than true. There is "cheap grace" and there is also cheap repentance in which we say not "I'm sorry I did it" but instead "I'm sorry I got caught." But we have to keep looking at Manasseh as a witness, a purveyor of truth. Manasseh is an example of genuine repentance in this story. When God effected redemption by restoring Manasseh to the throne of Judah, Manasseh was a changed person.

Manasseh didn't just make empty vows. He offered God honest entreaty and supplication as he was going through the process. The clear sign of the honesty of his repentance is that he followed through on his promises. He modified his ways. He changed his worship to the correct display of loving God. Formerly an idolater, he became a destroyer of idols. He had been a polytheist but became one who put away false gods, relegating them to the darkest recesses. Manasseh not only stopped worshiping his idols, he threw them away, reducing the temptation.

Manasseh had had no trouble identifying his idols. What are our idols today? We all have them, and they get us into trouble, like Manasseh's did. Whatever comes between us and God is an idol. We need to identify our idols in order to finally and decisively put them away. Manasseh destroyed his idols once he had turned to God. His action wasn't the cause of his receiving God's forgiveness but the result of that sympathy and grace. Manasseh wasn't trying to practice a works-based grace. He put away his idols in obedience to God, not as a payment or a trade-off. Manasseh's elimination of his idols was quite thorough. He didn't refrain from idolatry one day a week, or even six days a week. He got entirely rid of them. They weren't his "demons" anymore. His repentance wasn't merely intellectual, or even emotional, although it did involve those aspects. It entailed an earnest, exceptional deed: casting the idols out. Like all people who try to start fresh, he knew that true repentance is a change of mind which results in a change of behavior.

Manasseh's repentance didn't suddenly fix it all, though. He didn't become perfect. He still had some problems in that he was as of yet permitting the high places. Like Manasseh, we are still fallen, still sinners from the moment we are born, even if forgiven. But God showed Manasseh that slipping isn't total failure. When God's people struggle in the mire of evil, we are to say sorry and get back to work improving our behavior.

The results aren't easy, and they are not always obvious, or even visible. Manasseh didn't see even one of the great things he had a hand in. His grandson was Josiah, the greatest king after David, who ended Baal worship in Israel's official religion.

Coals From The Altar

A question often comes up in church and Bible classes: Why don't Christians offer sacrifice? Here is one of my favorite answers, offered by a grade schooler: Because we don't raise sheep anymore.

Of course, the real answer is: Jesus Christ was the ultimate, final sacrifice.

So why did Israel offer sacrifices in the Old Testament? Deuteronomy 16:16 commanded that sacrifice be offered three times a year, minimum, by each Israelite man. And in the New Testament temple, sacrifice was offered an astonishing three times a day.

Isaiah 6 gives us an important part of the larger answer why sacrifices were offered, but to understand the teaching about sacrifice in the chapter, we must first examine some background material and ideas. First let's look at the creation story where Genesis 2:17 and 3:6–7 and 21 contain the concept of sacrifice.

To review, in that section, God tells the man that eating fruit from the forbidden tree will result in death. (This is in concept similar to Paul's statement in Romans 6:23: "For the wages of sin is death," which is an Old Testament principle.) The man and the woman are deliberately disobedient. Had atonement not been extended by God, they would have died on the spot, just as God warned them.) But there is a cost. The animal that provided the skins for the humans' clothing had died. God would rather allow the unfairness of the innocent animal being killed than the death of the guilty people. This manifests a clear biblical principle: God loves people more than he loves animals. Sacrifice enabled Adam and Eve to continue to have a limited association with God.

Realize that God didn't want the animal to die, he wanted it to live a long life and produce offspring. Sacrifice was a loss to God instead of a gift. He forfeited one of the precious animals which he had created, but he gained in the transaction by not losing the humans, even if their quality of life would be reduced now.

Israel did not see sacrifice as a gift to God. We see this clearly in the book of Leviticus which contains several sets of instructions regarding the proper way to offer sacrifices and the role of the priests. While much of the instruction is straightforwardly procedural, we can also find theological explanation of the purpose of sacrifice. Leviticus 1:3–4 states clearly that the worshiper "shall offer it at the door of the tent of meeting, that he may be accepted before the LORD; he shall lay his hand upon the head of the burnt offering, and it shall be accepted for him to make atonement for him." The theory of the sacrifice is stated to be atonement for sin. Forgiveness of sin and restored relationship with God are the outcomes. The gift to God is the redeemed worshiper, not meat for God's table.

This is also evinced in Leviticus 5:10. The priest's offering of the worshipers' sacrifice "shall make atonement for him for the sin which he has committed, and he shall be forgiven." It's spiritual, though it looks like something physical—like appeasing God with food. But God does not eat animals, certainly not the ashes of animals. He tells Israel in Psalm 50:12–13, "If I were hungry, I would not tell you; for the world and all that is in it is mine. Do I eat the flesh of bulls, or drink the blood of goats?" and in verse 10, "For every beast of the forest is mine, the cattle on a thousand hills." So it's a tautology that God wants his own animals back through sacrifice. There's a different reason. Redemption can only come from God's grace which provides for sacrifice to effect atonement. "Without the shedding of blood there is no remission" of sin (Hebrews 9:22).

Our themes of covenant, sin, and redemption are very clear in the Israelite theology of sacrifice. God has a covenant with Israel, and the instructions and commands regarding sacrifice are an integral element of the covenant. Sacrifice is required because of human sin, and sacrifice, accompanied by repentance, brings God's redemption. This concept of sacrifice found in the Old Testament is clearly carried over into the New Testament and is the theological basis behind seeing Jesus's death as a sacrificial offering. This is stated most openly, if metaphorically, by John the Baptist in John 1:29: "Behold the Lamb of God, which taketh away the sins of the world." Jesus is the sacrificed Lamb, whose death brings about atonement for sin and restored relationship with God. Whereas animal sacrifice had to be offered repeatedly, Jesus was the ultimate and final one.

This background concerning sacrifice as understood in Israel is necessary for proper understanding of Isaiah 6. It's a very different kind of text than the other stories in our since it is a recounting of a vision. As such, it is not useful to perform normal historical studies on this story. The story can still be useful in piecing together the history of the theology of the temple, the development of Israelite theology, and the history of other such disciplines of the mind, but there are very few, if any, objective events to reconstruct from this text.

One solid historical fact which we find in the text is a date for the event—the year of the death of King Uzziah. So Isaiah's vision happened at a particular time in history, "in the year" God appeared to Isaiah. God is not defined by time, but he appears in it. The idea that God manifests himself in a chronological framework is related to the idea that God was at work in the national life, the history of his chosen people of Israel. The exodus, the crossing of the Red Sea, the conquest of Canaan, the reign of King David, the exile, and many other events related in the Old Testament are presented as mighty acts of God in history, in time. The historical element of Isaiah's vision is firmly in the line of God's acts in history. King Uzziah was the great, great, ever-so-great grandson of King David and the heir of God's promise to David of an eternal dynasty. God's faithfulness to the Zion/David covenant was clear in the presence of a descendant of David on the throne in Jerusalem.

While Isaiah's vision is not susceptible to normal historical inquiry, his call story still fits our overall purpose in that it is presented in story form and that Isaiah saw the things which he relates as events with duration, sequence, and meaning. It is not history, but it is a kind of story and can be interpreted as such. The meaning of the story will be our main focus in this section as it has been for each preceding chapter.

The first four verses of our text deal with the holiness of God and connect that sacred character with the temple in Jerusalem. The temple was seen as the center of God's presence in the earth. The big rock on which God stood to speak to David was likely the floor of the Holy of Holies where the ark of the covenant was kept. The ark, the big rock, and the Holy of Holies shared the distinction of containing God's spirit in a special way, and all were located in the rearmost room of the Jerusalem temple. When Isaiah was in the temple in his vision, he had some level of access to the Holy of Holies, and as a result he came into direct contact with God, seeing firsthand his sanctity.

Isaiah saw and heard the LORD. God revealed himself in comprehensible terms that Isaiah was able to understand without an angel to explain the vision as Daniel required. Isaiah doesn't describe what he *saw* except to say that God's train filled the temple, but he *heard* God communicate in intelligible human speech. God revealed himself in such a way that Isaiah was clear about the meaning of the message which God was sending.

Isaiah envisioned God as on a throne, which shows God's royal character. The throne was high and lifted up, which shows that God is above all, a symbolic statement of God as powerful, almighty. God was seen as occupying the temple, but it was only his train that was actually in the temple. The temple doesn't enclose God nor contain him. It had a direct connection to God and is holy as a result, but God is not limited to that location. He is present in the temple in a special way but not bound to it. Consequently, God is greater than the temple. He dwells in heaven, not in a physical building. God is everywhere and not limited to the temple but his presence is in the temple in a special way.

God occupying the temple is a sign of his covenant with Israel and the promise of his "being there" through thick or thin for his chosen people.

Like Ezekiel and John, Isaiah found that one of the dimensions of God's holiness was the unusual creatures surrounding him. In Isaiah's vision the creatures were the seraphim, fire beings of strange conformation. The seraphim are, apparently from Isaiah's perception, a type of angel or other heavenly being.

The association of God with fire creates some tension within some people who mostly connect fire with hell. Neither the fire that issues from God's throne in Daniel 7 nor the fire of the seraphim is the fire of hell, but holy, purifying fire. God is closely associated with fire several times in the Bible, in fact. The pillar of fire in Exodus is God's guidance to Israel. God comes to Mount Sinai in smoke and fire. The nature of God's fire is explained clearly in Malachi 3:2 which states, "For he is like a refiner's fire." Isaiah 1:25 makes a similar point. It says, "I will turn my hand against you and will smelt away your dross as with lye and remove all your alloy." In both of those verses, God uses fire as a purifying agent, transforming something bad into something good. This is like iron ore which is just red rocks which are of little use, but which when heated in a hot enough fire are transformed into iron. In the same way, God converts sinners who decide to believe.

This happened to Isaiah in our story. God came to him and changed him from a man of unclean lips into a prophet, speaking on God's direct behalf. God comes to all of humanity for the same purpose. He wants to transform us into members of his kingdom, his family.

Within Isaiah's vision, the seraphim perform a specific function, the articulation of God's holiness. Their cry of "holy, holy, holy"—the Trisagion in theological jargon—reflects and proclaims God's nature. The triple repetition is a symbolic statement of the completeness and infinite nature of the holiness of God. The next statement by the seraphim is also an important theological pronouncement. "The whole earth is full of his glory" is a statement that God's presence is centered in the temple with his people, but that accompaniment spills out into all the earth. There is no place where God is not or where his spirit cannot be felt.

The smoke which Isaiah saw fill the temple fits a pattern found in several biblical texts. The pillar of cloud which guided Israel in the wilderness functions as a visible sign of God's presence. In I Kings 9, at the dedication of the temple, a cloud filled the temple showing that "the glory of the LORD filled the house of the LORD" (I Kings 9:11). A similar idea is found in Revelation: "The temple was filled with smoke from the glory of God and from his power" (Revelation 15:8). All of these texts present the presence of God as smoke, fog, or a cloud, and the nebulosity of the image is a way of representing the insubstantial and supernatural nature of God.

Isaiah's vision of God as smoke bears a definite resemblance to the description of Mount Sinai in Exodus 19 which states, "And Mount Sinai was wrapped in smoke, because the Lord descended upon it in fire; and the smoke of it went up like the smoke of a kiln, and the whole mountain quaked greatly." In similar fashion,

Isaiah saw fire, smoke, and shaking foundations of the threshold, very much like Sinai, if on a smaller scale.

Isaiah's response to this vision of the majesty of God was completely appropriate. He confessed his own sinfulness, therefore strongly implying his unworthiness to witness the vision. God didn't correct him. We see a similar pattern elsewhere. When confronted by God in the whirlwind, Job repented of his sin and abased himself before God. Peter likewise confessed that he was a sinful man and unworthy of Christ's presence in Luke 5:8 when he recognized Jesus. Isaiah, Job, and Peter all saw their true nature in comparison to the perfect holiness of God and recognized their sin and unworthiness to being in his presence. Isaiah's cry of "Woe is me! for I am undone" is quite correct. The natural result of a sinful human seeing the LORD of Hosts directly would be the destruction of the sinner. But God has made provision so that death is not the winner. God gets the last word, and that word is grace.

As has been shown, the flaming one, the seraphim, takes a burning coal from the altar and uses it to purify Isaiah. The seraphim touches Isaiah's unclean lips and says, "Your guilt is taken away, and your sin forgiven." Fire from the altar does not burn or damage. Instead it cleanses, like a refiner's fire, smelting away the dross. It is not just any fire from which the flaming one takes the coal; it is the fire atop the altar on which the sacrifice is offered. It is the sacrifice which enables the cleansing fire. "It shall be to him for atonement" (Leviticus 1:4). It certainly was for Isaiah, and it was so for any Israelite who offered sacrifice along with confession and repentance as Isaiah did.This passage gives us a rather complete picture of the theology of sacrifice in Israel. As a reparation of sin, it was not a gift *to* God. God did not need the dead animal: Isaiah *desperately* needed it.

It is instructive to note that the seraph came to Isaiah. Grace is extended by God. Sinful humanity cannot come to God, so God comes to us. Our sinful, fallen state prevents us from being able to approach God, so God manifests love and grace by making the move. God's extending of his hand is to change us—to purify, cleanse, redeem, and fit us for his presence and a renewed, restored relationship with the LORD.

Isaiah became a great prophet and accomplished spectacular things for God, but it was not those stunning works which brought him redemption. The works which Isaiah performed were not the cause of his redemption but the result of it. He was forgiven by God's grace not by works. Paul didn't invent that idea. His statement in Ephesians 2:8-9," For by grace you have been saved through faith; -- not because of works, lest any man should boast," is a statement of the Israelite theology found in Isaiah 6. Because Isaiah received mercy, he could come into God's presence, not as a sinner, but as a righteous member of God's family. After receiving his new status, Isaiah could see God without fear and hear God speak. No longer a foul-mouthed sinner, this prophet was confidently standing before God. Sin had no more hold on Isaiah. He remained there before God as if he had never sinned, as if he were perfectly righteous. God kept his covenant and extended grace and atonement for sin, bestowing unearned redemption on Isaiah.

Isaiah discovered quickly that he had been redeemed for a purpose. He was immediately commissioned as a prophet and told to go and speak God's words to Israel. God provided Isaiah with a call. Isaiah accepted that call. "Here am I. Send me," he replied. Redemption led Isaiah to being given a job by God, a job which Isaiah accepted and performed to the best of his ability. So overall, Isaiah got it right. He was a sinner who deserved eternal death, but through sacrifice and grace he was given mercy. In response he went to work, serving and obeying God.

You are equally a sinner, also deserving of eternal death. Through the death of Jesus Christ, you can be forgiven and receive eternal, abundant life. What do you need to do about that? What are *you* being called to do?

SDG

Printed in the United States
By Bookmasters